FAMILY WALKS
IN THE DOWNS AND VALES
OF WILTSHIRE

Nigel Vile

Scarthin Books, Cromford, Derbyshire   1988

FAMILY WALKS
IN THE DOWNS AND VALES
OF WILTSHIRE

Family Walks Series
General Editor: Norman Taylor

———

THE COUNTRY CODE
Guard against all risk of fire
Fasten all gates
Keep dogs under proper control
Keep to paths across farm land
Avoid damaging fences, hedges and walls
Leave no litter
Safeguard water supplies
Protect wildlife, wild plants and trees
Go carefully along country roads
Respect the life of the countryside

———

Published by Scarthin Books, Cromford, Derbyshire

Phototypesetting, printing by Higham Press Ltd., Shirland, Derbyshire

ISBN 0 907758 21 5

KENNET AND AVON CANAL, WILCOT (Route 3)

Preface

If you enjoy peace and solitude, Wiltshire is an ideal county. The majority of tourists simply pass by, on their way to the crowded beaches of Devon and Cornwall, and the South Coast, with little more than a cursory glance at the landscape. Apart from the vastly over-rated pile of stones at Stonehenge, nowadays totally overwhelmed by coach parties of visitors, Wiltshire is a little-known and infrequently explored county. Its real asset for the walker is that few tourists come to stay, which means that you really can have a peaceful and relaxed day-out in the countryside. In one sense this is surprising, since we have here scenery arguably unrivalled in southern England. The local landscape can match anything to be found in the North or South Downs, for example, but without the hordes that throng Box Hill or Leith Hill in Surrey on a summer's weekend. With these thoughts in mind, I commend these walks to you as a gentle introduction to one of England's most ancient and historic counties.

Acknowledgements

I would like to thank Mandy Schmidt of Corsham in Wiltshire for the fine sketches which illustrate some of the walks. Thanks are also due to my wife, Gill, for her patience, my daughters Laura and Katie for their endurance, and son James, whose experience of walking has so far been from the confines of a back-pack.

About the Author

Nigel Vile was born in Bristol. He lives in Bradford-on-Avon and teaches Economics and Environmental Studies at Corsham School, Wiltshire. His enthusiasm and enjoyment derive from field-study trips with his pupils and family walking with his wife and three children. The success of his first book, **Family Walks around Bristol, Bath and the Mendips**, showed how well he could infect others with delight in country walking.

2

CONTENTS

WILTSHIRE.

GLOUCESTERSHIRE

OXFORDSHIRE

SWINDON
⊙
1. Barbury Castle

MALMESBURY

AVON

CHIPPENHAM
⊙

2. Fyfield Down

BERKSHIRE

4. Avebury ⊙ MARLBOROUGH

6. Cherhill

5. Pewsey Vale

7. Oliver's
   Castle

3. Wilcot
⊙ PEWSEY

⊙
TROWBRIDGE

SALISBURY

PLAIN

8. Westbury

SOMERSET

9. Cley Hill
⊙ WARMINSTER

10. Scratchbury
    Hill

11. Stonehenge

HAMPSHIRE

15. Cold
    Kitchen
    Hill

13. Grovely
    Wood

12. Old Sarum

16. White
    Sheet
    Hill

⊙ MERE

14. Forant

⊙ SALISBURY

DORSET

SCALE

0   10   20 MILES

4

Introduction

Welcome to this collection of walks written with the family very much in mind! Too many walking guides have routes that average out at between 5 and 10 miles in length, with quite severe gradients and rough terrain. This book, to quote a phrase, will hopefully prove to be 'something completely different'. The length of each walk has been kept deliberately short, the average distance being 3½ miles, in order that a normal fit youngster can complete the distance. As far as possible, you will find that a pub or tea-shop will either await you en route, or at the end of a walk, failing which a choice of fine picnicking sites has been indicated. Road-walking is kept to an absolute minimum, although many of the walks criss-cross roads to facilitate the rescue of tired youngsters (or parents!) should the need arise. To add interest for youngsters, each walk contains a number of suitable attractions. It may be a chambered long barrow, possibly a chalk stream suitable for paddling, or perhaps a rich variety of flora to identify. Finally, each route is circular to avoid any retracing of steps.

The expression 'as different as chalk and cheese' describes Wiltshire perfectly, for here are two distinct landscapes. There is firstly the chalk downland, rising to almost 1000 feet at Tan Hill, east of Devizes. Below the chalk hills lie the clay vales, rich dairying and arable pastures that border rivers like the Wylye, the Kennet and the Avon. The chalk downland is perhaps Wiltshire's most well-known natural feature, peppered with rich natural history and ancient archaeological sites. Many of Britain's most famous prehistoric remains are here: vast stone circles at Stonehenge and Avebury; ancient hill-forts at Old Sarum and White Sheet Hill; West Kennet with its long barrow; and the Wansdyke, an ancient line of defence. Cley Hill near Warminster is a mecca for UFO spotters; above Bratton and Westbury white horses gleam on the chalk hillsides; scattered across Fyfield Down lie ancient sarsen stones. It is a curious and mysterious landscape, the heart of historic Wessex, that these Family Walks explore.

Choosing a walk.

Never throw inexperienced youngsters "in at the deep end" when walking! Rutted tracks and slippery downland slopes are far harder going than the pavement that leads to the manicured lawns of the local park. Routes 1, 6, 7 and 14 make ideal introductory half-day rambles. On more strenuous routes, a good idea is to make contingency plans so that if the party gets part-way, and exhausted youngsters think that going to the dentist is preferable to walking, rescue can be arranged by meeting friends with transport at a suitable point, or by a driver hurrying back to collect the car. In the appendices, I have made a subjective assessment of the routes in order of difficulty, to help you choose.

Allowing sufficient time.

Each walk is intended to take up the best part of a half or whole day, allowing time for play, exploration and rest. It is better to over-estimate rather than under-estimate the time required, thus avoiding the need to have to 'route march' the latter part of the journey. As a rough guide, allow a pace of around one mile per hour for very young children, graduating to two miles per hour for the experienced ten-year-old.

What to wear.

It should go without saying that, given the British climate, it is advisable to go walking prepared for the worst! Proper walking-boots or stout shoes are preferable to wellington boots, which are fine for walking the dog in the park but are tiring and rub on more serious walks. Following a spell of dry weather, the quality of Wiltshire's chalk tracks and paths make trainers a feasible option on these shorter walks. On top, I prefer several thin layers that can gradually be peeled off as it gets warmer, rather than one thick jumper that just gives the hot/cold options! Waterproof cagoules are a must, too. Cords are better than jeans, the latter being extremely uncomfortable when wet due to their 'clinginess'. A cap or bobble-hat is also useful during colder weather, bearing in mind that the crown of the head is where the body's greatest heat-loss will occur. Don't forget a small rucksack for all those items that make a walk that much more enjoyable - picnics, maps, cameras, spotter guides, towels and so on.

Route-finding.

The maps in this book, taken in conjuction with the directions supplied, should prove more than adequate when it comes to route finding. All rights of way have been followed as far as possible according to the line shown on Ordnance Survey 1:50,000 Landranger maps. In some cases, where a right of way has been shown as crossing a field which is now ploughed or sown, the path has been altered to go round the edge of the field. Needless to say, if you find such an obstacle, make an appropriate detour. The vast majority of the routes in this book will be following clearly defined paths with no such difficulties. For those who like to carry O.S. maps when out walking, the following sheets cover the relevant walks.

Routes 1-7	Sheet 173	Swindon and Devizes
Routes 9, 15, 16	Sheet 183	Yeovil and Frome
Routes 8, 10-14	Sheet 184	Salisbury and the Plain

Refreshments

I have indicated where public-houses, cafes and tea-rooms can be found on the walks. Most of the pubs en route allow children accompanied by adults on to their premises, usually into adjoining gardens.

Teashop opening times vary according to the time of year and expected custom, but most can be relied upon to stay open until five or six o'clock during the summer months. Where no refreshment stops are found on the route itself, I have suggested picnic spots or convenient hostelries in the immediate area.

Conclusion.

Do not forget the Country Code. Ramblers need the farmer as their friend, not their enemy, and it is our duty to cultivate a responsible attitude towards the countryside both in our children and ourselves. Finally, I wish you as much pleasure in walking these routes as I had in preparing them. Good walking!

LADIES' BRIDGE (Route 3)

7

Symbols used on the route maps

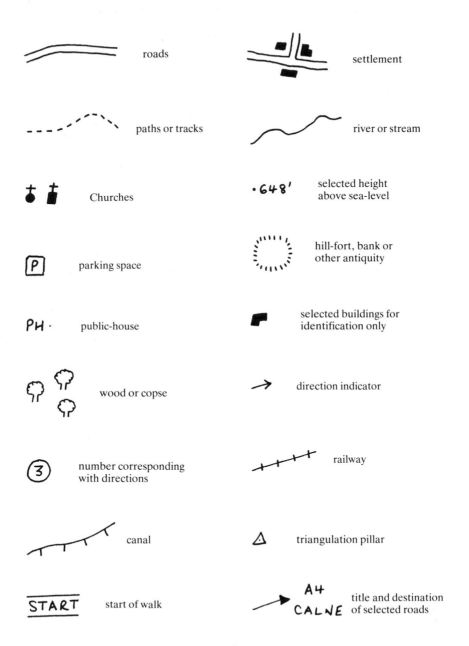

roads	settlement
paths or tracks	river or stream
Churches	•648' selected height above sea-level
P parking space	hill-fort, bank or other antiquity
PH · public-house	selected buildings for identification only
wood or copse	→ direction indicator
3 number corresponding with directions	railway
canal	△ triangulation pillar
START start of walk	A4 CALNE title and destination of selected roads

Barbury Castle and the Ridgeway

Outline   Barbury Castle ~ The Ridgeway ~ Barbury Castle.

Summary   Each major town has its 'playground' and the Barbury Castle Country Park fulfils this role for Swindon, the largest settlement in Wiltshire and allegedly the fastest growing town within the EEC. Sited high on the Marlborough Downs, with fine views in all directions, this walk includes a stretch of the Ridgeway long-distance path. The paths are well-used, and hence clearly defined, ending with a fairly steep ascent to regain the heights of Barbury Castle.

Attractions   Barbury Castle is an Iron Age hill-fort, with two ramparts and accompanying ditches enclosing a site of some 11½ acres. Evidence would suggest that the enclosure was occupied as a town, with aerial photography revealing huts and storage pits. This must have been a tremendously strong hillfort, with any prospective invaders facing strenuous hillside climbing before reaching the site breathless and unfit for battle. Just south of Barbury Castle, the OS. map shows a battlefield site sandwiched between a wood and a country lane. The battle was Beranburh, fought in 556 AD., when 'Cynric and Caewlin fought against the Britons' (Anglo Saxon Chronicle).

Below Barbury Castle, the Ridgeway descends gently to the clay vale. All around lies rich arable farmland, with the landscape a sea of ripening crops in mid-summer. The two most common cereals are wheat and barley, the latter distinguishable by its tufted heads. Whereas wheat is grown mainly for making bread, barley is used for feeding farm animals and brewing.

Towards the end of the walk, a Sarsen Stone monument has been erected in memory of Wiltshire's great pastoral writers, Richard Jefferies and Alfred Williams. Jefferies, a one-time reporter on the North Wiltshire Herald, wrote many books that drew heavily on the people, places and natural history of his beloved Downland. Williams was more of a poet, whose spare time was spent walking the local hills and breathing in their unique atmosphere. The monument records two inscriptions:

Alfred Williams   *Richard Jefferies*
1877 - 1930   *1848 - 1887*
Still to find and still to follow   *It is Eternity now.*
Joy in every hill and hollow   *I am in the midst*
Company in solitude.   *of it. It is about*
                    me in the sunshine.   *continued on page 12*

9

Route 1

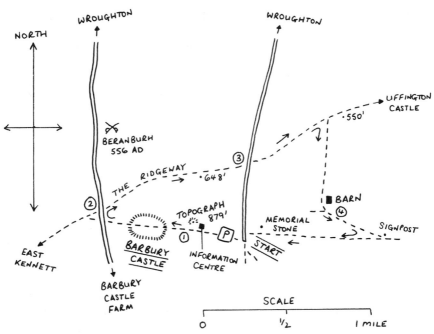

JEFFERIES MONUMENT

Route 1

Barbury Castle and the Ridgeway   3 miles

START   *Three miles south of Swindon, the A361 Devizes road passes through Wroughton. At the mini-roundabout in the centre of the village, follow the sign for the Barbury Castle Country Park. Four miles from Wroughton, at the top of a steep hill, the lane ends in the Country Park parking area. (GR. 157761).*

ROUTE

1. *Take the path to the left of the Information Centre that heads out to Barbury Castle. Either take the path through the centre of the Castle, or follow the top of the southern ramparts. You eventually reach a country lane.*

2. *Turn right, and a few yards down the hill the Ridgeway path forks off on the right-hand side. Follow this path for one mile to another country lane.*

3. *A little way down the lane to your left, the Ridgeway continues on its way towards Uffington Castle. Continue along the path for half-a-mile, and then take a field path on your right-hand side. A barn at the far end of this field path will indicate that you are on the correct route.*

4. *Immediately past the barn, bear left and take the path that gradually ascends the hillside. After half-a-mile, at a signpost, turn right following the signed route uphill towards Barbury Castle. Just beyond the Memorial Stone, you reach the lane that leads into the parking area.*

Public Transport Thamesdown Transport run regular buses to Wroughton village and the RAF Hospital halfway between the village and Barbury Castle.

It is worth returning to the Information Centre at the end of the walk to discover more information about the local landscape - its flora and fauna, its history and its archaeology. There are also detailed displays about both Jefferies and Williams. Close by is a viewpoint and topograph, detailing obvious landmarks such as Wroughton Airfield (2 miles) and Uffington Castle (11 miles), as well as less well-know points such as the Creamery Chimney at Latton (19 miles)!

Refreshments   All around the Barbury Castle Country Park site there are excellent picnicking spots. Just adjacent to the parking area there is a properly equipped picnic site. Back in the village of Wroughton, there are several pubs including the Three Tuns and the White Hart.

FYFIELD CHURCH

Route 2

Fyfield Down and the Sarsen Stones

Outline   Fyfield ~ Fyfield Down ~ Devil's Den ~ Clatford Bottom ~ Fyfield.

Summary   A pleasing walk that provides a good introduction to the North Wessex Downs between Avebury and Marlborough. The generally flat lanes, field paths and tracks cross a landscape littered with ancient Sarsen Stones and modern race horse training courses. A large part of the walk lies within the Fyfield Down National Nature Reserve, resulting in a rich flora and fauna largely undisturbed by modern farming methods.

Attractions   An astute member of my family commented that interesting walks often have unpromising beginnings. That is a fair comment about this particular walk, with the first half-mile taking us from some rather ordinary village buildings, across the busy A4 and along a somewhat dull country lane that leads to a farm. Don't be tempted to give up though, because beyond the farm a fascinating walk begins to develop. The enclosed grass track from this farm brings you to the Fyfield Down National Nature Reserve. This is one of the largest Downland tracts containing sarsen deposits within Britain, that is actively conserved and farmed as it has been for many centuries. Here are few traces of the modern arable farming practices that have changed the character of so much traditional Downland. Within the Reserve, the ornithologist within your group will constantly be scanning the sky. The resident bird population includes sparrowhawks, kestrels and long-eared owls, with buzzards, red kites and stone curlews being listed amongst the occasional visitors.

Within the Reserve, a valley floor strewn with Sarsen Stones is passed. These stones are also known as Grey Wethers, wethers being a name for sheep, which these 'remnants of a siliceous duricrust layer' resemble. This was megalithic man's building material, the great stones of Stonehenge, for example, being sarsens from the Marlborough Downs. So numerous are these stones and boulders, youngsters will undoubtedly use them as stepping stones, seeing how far they can walk without touching the turf.

On the gentle hillside slopes, posts and carefully mown grass strips mark the race-horse training courses that lie hereabouts. Many an Ascot or Aintree winner has been trained on the Wiltshire and Berkshire

continued on page 16

13

Route 2

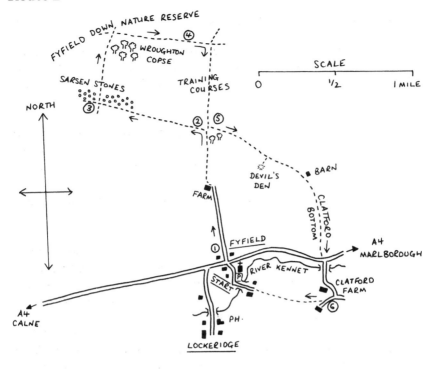

THE DEVIL'S DEN

14

Route 2

Fyfield Down and the Sarsen Stone   5 miles

START   *The village of Fyfield lies 3 miles west of Marlborough on the main A4 road. There is room for sensible parking by St. Nicholas Church, which lies down a lane to the south of the A4. (GR. 148687).*

ROUTE

1. *Walk back to the A4, and follow the lane directly opposite signposted to Temple Bottom. After ½ mile, the lane ends at a farm. Cross a gate directly ahead, and follow an enclosed grass track downhill to a clump of trees.*

2. *At the clump of trees, go left and follow the course of the hedgerow. Eventually, Sarsen Stones begin to appear in the valley bottom, which becomes the most interesting route to follow.*

3. *A little way along the valley, a gateway is reached. The stones continue on ahead, but our path is to the right. A succession of gateways are passed before the path clips the western edge of Wroughton Copse. Just beyond the end of the copse, a gateway brings you on to the hilltop. Turn right, and follow the hilltop fence.*

4. *Eventually, a Nature Reserve information boards marks the end of the reserve. The path continues straight ahead across open fields with no obvious pathway! Fortunately, blue-topped marker posts indicate the route. A hilltop sign, alongside an upright sarsen, marks a crossroads of footpaths. Turn right and head downhill, following the path marked to Fyfield. Again, blue-topped posts mark the route across the race-horse training courses.*

5. *The downhill path eventually emerges by the clump of trees passed earlier in the walk. If the party is tired, then simply retrace your steps back to Fyfield. Our walk now goes left, and you head for the gateway at the far side of the field. This gateway marks yet another boundary of the Nature Reserve, as a board indicates. At the gateway, carry straight on following the obvious path through Clatford Bottom and on to the A4. Naturally, you will want to cross into the field containing the Devil's Den for a short detour.*

6. *Cross the A4 and follow the private lane signposted to Clatford Farm. The lane passes behind the farmhouse, and a T-junction is soon reached where the route bears right. A signpost and a stile indicate the footpath back to Fyfield, which follows the only obvious route.*

Public Transport This is a remote and sparsely populated part of Wiltshire, with very little by way of regular and reliable public transport. A car is essential.

Downs. Walkers will rarely encounter a Red Rum or a Shergar, however, with the workouts and exercises taking place long before most of us have breakfasted!

Lying in a field just by Clatford Bottom is the Devil's Den. This is a megalithic burial chamber consisting of four large base stones topped off with a capstone, a lump of sarsen three feet thick and ten feet square. The mound of this long barrow has almost disappeared. It is strange to find such an ancient relic, very similar to a Welsh-style Cromlech, lying in a valley instead of on the more usual skyline location. It remains a fascinating site that youngsters will thoroughly enjoy exploring.

The River Kennet is crossed twice towards the end of the walk. It is just possible to crawl down to the river bank in Fyfield itself, and enjoy a paddle in the river's clear cool waters. Less agile members of your group will have to be satisfied with the view from the bridge. It should be possible to spot the red-beaked moorhen, although being a nervous creature it will quickly dive for cover into the vegetation along the river bank. When I was here in early July, there were several small fluffy chicks, with prominent red beaks, accompanying mum on her travels up and down the river, a sight that youngsters will really enjoy seeing.

Refreshments Very close to the start of the walk is the village of Lockeridge (see the map). In the village, there is the 'Who'd a thought it' public house, which serves meals and snacks. On the walk, the valley containing the bulk of the Sarsen Stones or the Devil's Den site make excellent picnic spots where youngsters will find plenty to amuse them.

Route 3 5 miles

Woodborough, Wilcot and the Kennet and Avon Canal

Outline Woodborough ~ Wilcot ~ Kennet and Avon Canal ~ Woodborough Hill ~ Woodborough.

Summary The route follows flat field paths, lanes and a canal towpath between Woodborough and Wilcot, two attractive villages in the heart of the Vale of Pewsey. The walk to Wilcot is pleasant, if unspectacular, with the return along the canal towpath containing much of interest. A one-mile detour at the end of the walk to the top of Woodborough Hill provides some exhilarating views of the locality.

Attractions Two of the farmer's greatest pests are the wood-pigeon and the rabbit, both of whom enjoy a diet of grasses, corn and vegetables. The tree-lined hedgerow that borders the field-path between Woodborough and Swanborough Tump provides the ideal habitat for both these creatures, giving them protection close to their many sources of food. It is little wonder that pigeon-pie and rabbit casserole have frequented rural table-tops over many centuries!

A plaque by the roadside marks the spot known as Swanborough Tump, described as the 'meeting place of the hundred of Swanborough'. This was reputed to be the seat of a Saxon hundred court where Ethelred and Alfred the Great held a state council. One source even suggests that Alfred made his will on this site. I searched in vain for the Bronze Age round barrow on which they met, but unless it lay under the waist-deep nettles beyond the plaque, it has probably met the same fate as many of Wiltshire's other smaller antiquities - the farmer's plough. The site of Swanborough Tump is something of a disappointment.

Wilcot is a picturesque village. The Church is worth exploring, with its ancient scratch dial against which to check the accuracy of your timepiece, but undoubtedly the highlight of the village it its profusion of thatched cottages. Thatched roofs will last up to 60 years if made from traditional reed, although today the cheaper long straw, with a life of some 20 years, is more common. It is estimated that there are some 500 thatchers in Britain today servicing the country's 50,000 thatched cottages. Look out for the thatcher's mark as you pass through Wilcot, a decoration in the shape of a bird or animal made of straw.

The Kennet and Avon Canal between Wilcot and Woodborough contains the unique stretch of water known as 'Wilton Wide Water'.

continued on page 20

Route 3

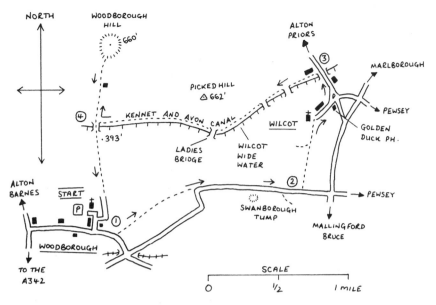

THATCHED COTTAGE, WILCOT

Route 3

Woodborough, Wilcot and the Kennet and Avon Canal

3 miles

START *From Devizes, a minor road leads to Alton Barnes, where a right turn takes you to Woodborough. A left-turn in the village brings you to the lane that leads to the Church, outside of which is a parking space. (GR. 114600).*

ROUTE

1. *Turn left at the bottom of the lane that leads away from the Church. Shortly, on a bend, take the path sign-posted 'Swanborough Tump'. This path crosses several fields, with the hedgerow always being kept immediately to your left. Where the road is joined, continue straight on, passing Swanborough Tump.*

2. *A few yards past the track that leaves the road on the right-hand side, two close gateways appear in the left-hand hedgerow. From the second of these, Wilcot Church comes into view. Pass through the gateway, and the right of way is down the left-hand side of the field. Continue on to Wilcot village, the field path eventually joining a farm track.*

3. *Having passed through Wilcot as shown on the map, pick up the canal towpath which is followed for close on 2 miles back towards Woodborough.*

4. *At Woodborough Fields Bridge, the towpath changes banks, and here you have the option of climbing to the top of Woodborough Hill before returning to your vehicle, all along the clear farm tracks indicated on the map.*

Public Transport The Wiltshire and Dorset Bus Company operate an infrequent service between Devizes and Pewsey that passes through Woodborough.

Tradition maintains that Lady Wroughton, owner of Wilcot Manor, would only agree to the canal passing through the Manor grounds if it were cut in the form of a wooded ornamental lake. To perfect the scene, an ornately carved bridge, Ladies Bridge, was erected at the western end of the Wide Water. The flora and fauna of the canal bank is something rather special, too. In season, this stretch of water can boast moorhen and reed warbler, bullrushes and yellow flag, as well as the ubiquitous dragon-fly.

It is worth walking to the top of Woodborough Hill at the end of the walk. In June, the rich flora that bedecks this chalk hillock contains such unusual species as the alpine milk vetch and the spotted orchis. The views of the surrounding countryside are breathtaking as well. To the north-west lie the Wessex Downs, with Wiltshire's highest point, Tan Hill, being especially prominent, along with the Alton Barnes White Horse. To the south lies the Vale of Pewsey, with the upland region of Salisbury Plain away in the distance.

Refreshments The Golden Duck Public House in Wilcot doubles-up as the village shop. There are tables and chairs on the grass outside the pub, where families could enjoy a drink.

AVEBURY STONE CIRCLE

Avebury, Silbury Hill and the Ridgeway.

Outline   Avebury ~ Silbury Hill ~ West Kennet Long Barrow ~ Overton Hill ~ The Ridgeway ~ Avebury.

Summary   Relatively flat tracks and paths that pass amongst one of the most ancient and mysterious landscapes in Britain. The imprints of ancient civilisation are everywhere - stone circles, a long barrow, round barrows, ancient trackways and unexplained mounds.

Attractions   That this is important countryside for the archaeologist is clear from the fact that three of the monuments on this walk receive a mention in the Guinness Book of Records. The earthworks and stone circles at Avebury are described as 'Britain's largest megalithic prehistoric monument', Silbury Hill is renowned for being 'the largest artificial mound in Europe' and the West Kennet Long Barrow is 'England's longest barrow containing a megalithic chamber'. Learned academics have written lengthy tomes on these strange and mysterious landmarks, speculating as to their origins and functions. It is a literature that I feel quite incapable of adding to. Suffice to say that at each site there is an informative plaque from which the interested observer can learn more, whilst at Avebury a selection of excellent literature can be purchased. Michael Pitts' volume 'Footprints through Avebury' is a fine guide for the interested layman.

    This concentration of ancient landmarks is added to by the site of the Sanctuary on Overton Hill, a Bronze Age Stone Circle which was unfortunately removed by an 18th century builder for 'a dirty little profit'. The stones, whose location is now indicated by plain concrete pillars, probably form the wall of some unsuspecting person's cottage in Avebury village. Alongside the Sanctuary lies a fine collection of Round Barrows, whose excavation revealed amongst other things a crouched skeleton, a bronze dagger and axe, and a coffin shaped from a hollow tree trunk. Despite all of these archaeological wonders, I am certain that the memory that will linger longest with any youngsters is the internal exploration of the Long Barrow at West Kennet. Don't spoil the fun by forgetting to bring a torch with you!

    Our constant companion throughout the early part of the walk is the River Kennet. The Kennet, a clear chalk stream where water cress abounds, has its source near to Avebury, before flowing on through Marlborough and Newbury to join the Thames at Reading. Between

continued on page 24

Route 4

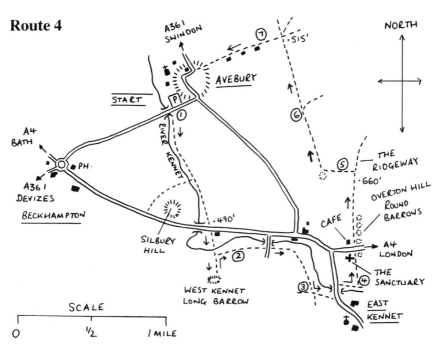

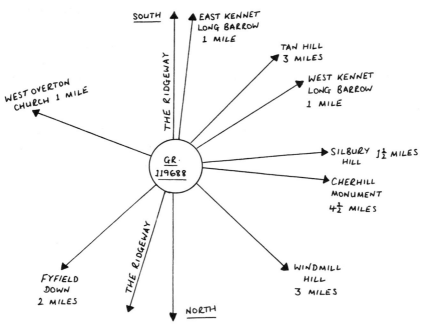

22

Route 4

Avebury, Silbury Hill and the Ridgeway 4 miles

START   *Avebury lies one mile north of the A4 at Beckhampton, on the A361 Devizes to Swindon road. There is a public car-park on the southern outskirts of the village.* (GR. 101697).

ROUTE

1. *Cross the A361, and follow the footpath sign-posted 'West Kennet Long Barrow'. This path borders the River Kennet all of the way to the A4, where a short detour to the foot of Silbury Hill is worthwhile. At the A4, cross the main road and follow the way-marked path to the long barrow. Retrace your steps to the foot of the enclosed path that led to the barrow, and take the stile on your right into the adjoining field.*

2. *Follow the right of way along the left-hand boundary fence. A track is soon joined that is followed on to a country lane. Cross this lane into the field ahead, where the public right of way follows the right-hand boundary fence. Follow the path through two fields, over a stile and continue along an enclosed, and normally overgrown, path.*

3. *At a staggered crossroads of paths, turn left and continue on to the lane that leads to East Kennet. Turn left, cross the river, and then turn right immediately into a field.*

4. *The public right of way follows the right-hand boundary, a gate is reached in quarter of a mile, and beyond the gateway a left-turn heading towards the A4 at Overton Hill is taken. Cross the A4 and continue ahead on the Ridgeway.*

5. *After half a mile, take a path to the left.*

6. *Leave the obvious track where it bears right up the hillside, instead climb the gate straight ahead and follow the right-hand boundary fence across several fields.*

7. *Another half-mile of field path brings you to a wide track, where you turn left and walk the remaining few hundred yards back into Avebury village.*

Public Transport   The regular Badgerline service from Swindon to Devizes passes through Avebury village.

Newbury and Reading, sections of the river have been canalized and it consequently lends its name to one of Britain's more well-known waterways - the Kennet and Avon Canal. I would be most surprised if the average youngster is not asking to paddle in the Kennet's inviting waters within half a mile of leaving the Avebury carpark. Despite being early on in the walk, it is worth acceding to their demands since the river is most accessible at this point.

The Ridgeway is one of Britain's officially designated long-distance footpaths. It is made up of two ancient trackways, the Great Ridgeway and the Icknield Way. The Great Ridgeway ran from Overton Hill to the Thames at Streatley, following the chalk ridge of the Marlborough Downs and the Berkshire Downs, whilst the Icknield Way continued from the opposite bank of the Thames at Goring, across the Chiltern Hills, and on to Ivinghoe Beacon in Hertfordshire. The Ridgeway is possibly the path to think about when initiating youngsters into the art of long-distance walking. Not only is it flat and well-served by small country towns and villages, but also it is relatively short, being just 85 miles in length from Overton to Ivinghoe. This compares favourably with other long-distance paths such as the 251 miles of the Pennine Way and the 510 miles of the South West Costal Path! Running along the edge of a chalk ridge, it provides immense views without any of the switch-back climbing associated with other long-distance paths.

Where our path leaves the Ridgeway, it is worth looking back towards the south to appreciate the fine view of this historic slice of the Wessex landscape. With the help of the topograph it should be possible to pick-out the many local landmarks, including the highest point in Wiltshire, Tan Hill, at just under 1000 feet above sea-level.

Refreshments   Half-way around the walk, on the A4 at Overton Hill, is the Ridgeway transport cafe. In Avebury itself is the Red Lion Inn and Stones Restaurant.

The Pewsey Downs Nature Reserve
and the Wansdyke

Outline   Adam's Grave ~ Milk Hill ~ The Wansdyke ~ The Ridgeway
~ Adam's Grave.

Summary   This walk lies entirely above the 700 feet contour line, as it
crosses perhaps the finest Downland within North Wessex. The views are
vast, and the greater part of the landscape unspoiled by modern farming
techniques, due to its Nature Reserve status. The going is generally
straightforward, with just one steep ascent to Adam's Grave at the
outset, but this high open terrain remains best tackled on a clear, dry day
when the exceptional views can be fully appreciated.

Attractions   The Pewsey Downs National Nature Reserve lies on a steep
south-facing scarp slope that runs along the northern side of the Pewsey
Vale. The views to the south extend across the Vale to Salisbury Plain,
whilst to the north lies Silbury Hill and the countryside beyond. This is
one of the largest Downland sites now left free from the arable farmer's
plough. The flora of this upland landscape draws botanists from far and
wide, with species such as the burnt and bee orchid, the chalk milkwort,
the bastard-toadflax and the field fleawort all being residents of this
protected environment. The flowers in turn attract many grassland
butterflies, such as the chalk hill, common and small blues, marbled
whites and several skippers. A good spotter's handbook to both wild
flowers and butterflies is a must on this walk, but beware of grown adults
on their hands-and-knees muttering strange expressions like 'orchis
maculata' and 'polygala vulgaris'.

Adam's Grave is a late Neolithic long barrow, 200 feet long, 100 feet
wide and 20 feet high. Excavations in the 19th century revealed several
skeletons and a leaf arrowhead. This is said to be the site of a battle in 592
AD. between the Saxons of Wessex and those of Ceawlin of the Upper
Thames Valley. The Anglo Saxon Chronicle records a 'great slaughter'
here, a far cry from the peaceful spot that Adam's Grave is today, set high
on the hilltops with commanding views over the Pewsey Vale.

The Alton Barnes White Horse, 650 feet above sea-level, is said to
be visible from Old Sarum near Salisbury, some 20 miles away. It was cut
in 1812, at the expense of a Mr. Robert Pile of Alton Barnes, who paid a
journeyman painter £20 to carry out the task. John Thorpe, nicknamed

continued on page 28

Route 5

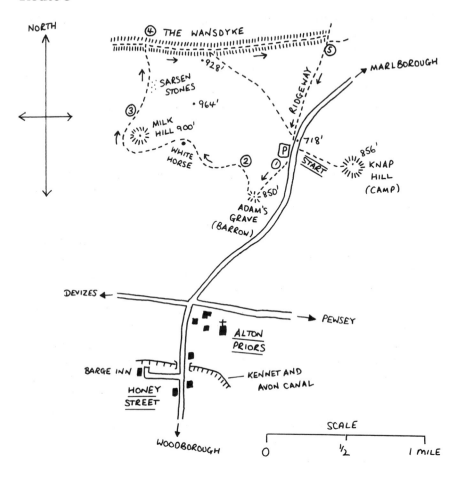

NORTH

④ THE WANSDYKE ⑤

•928'

SARSEN STONES

•964'

③ MILK HILL 900'

WHITE HORSE

② ①

RIDGEWAY

MARLBOROUGH

P 718'

START

850'

ADAM'S GRAVE (BARROW)

856'
KNAP HILL (CAMP)

DEVIZES ← → PEWSEY

ALTON PRIORS

BARGE INN

HONEY STREET

KENNET AND AVON CANAL

WOODBOROUGH

SCALE

0   ½   1 MILE

26

Route 5

The Pewsey Downs Nature Reserve and the Wansdyke

3 miles

START *Take the minor road from Devizes to Alton Priors, where you turn left at the crossroads and drive uphill on to the Downs. Park almost at the top, in the layby on your left, and walk about 40 yards back down the hill to a stile and a National Nature Reserve notice.* (GR. 115635).

ROUTE

1. *From the information board, Adam's Grave lies on the top of the hill that overlooks you. There is no obvious path, so simply make a short, sharp ascent of the hillside.*

2. *From Adam's Grave, follow the well-trodden Downland path towards the wooded summit of Milk Hill. The White Horse lies beyond the first hillside, and the path passes directly above this chalk hill figure. At Milk Hill, the path bears northwards around the hilltop. Wiltshire's highest point, Tan Hill, is clearly visible just to the west.*

3. *Follow the well-used hilltop path through a couple of gateways and then on to the Wansdyke, a clear ditch-and-bank earthwork.*

4. *Follow the Wansdyke eastwards for a mile or so until it joins the Ancient Ridgeway, avoiding one tempting right turn shown on the map. The last quarter of a mile of the Wansdyke is heavily overgrown, and it is necessary to follow the edge of either of the fields that border this linear earthwork.*

5. *Follow the Ancient Ridgeway, a well-defined track, southwards for the last half-mile back to the road. The final one hundred yards to the road is actually a field path.*

Public Transport The only buses that operate in this remote part of rural Wiltshire are infrequent services for schools and works. A car is therefore essential.

Jack the Painter, was foolishly paid in advance. He promptly disappeared! He was later hanged for some unknown crime, leaving Pile the task of finishing the horse himself. Such is the stuff of which legends are made!

Within this ancient landscape, natural deposits of sarsen boulders occur, the most famous being on nearby Fyfield Down (see walk 2). A few isolated sarsens, from which the megalithic builders took their stone, can be seen just to the north of Milk Hill. Sarsens are 'the remnants of a siliceous duricrust layer which formed on an eocene surface in the early tertiary some 70 million years ago' - quite so! In centuries past, the stone was hauled many miles to create stone circles and long barrow entrances. Today, at this spot, it provides a useful seat to rest on and marvel at the hang gliders that take off from the neighbouring hillside.

The Wansdyke, a linear frontier of bank and ditch, was built in the 6th or 7th century by the Britons, to act as a defence against invading pagan Saxons. It was probably successful in achieving this aim since no pagan Saxon burials have been found south of this line. To walk the line of the Wansdyke high up on the Wessex Downs has been described as 'one of the most spectacular experiences in British field archaeology', a statement with which I cannot but agree. It is a fine location for youngsters to burn up excess energy, acting out ancient invasions from the north, whilst the more sedentary can simply sit and breathe in the atmosphere of this ancient landscape.

Refreshments At the end of the walk, drive back to Honey Street a couple of miles to the south, where the Barge Inn is a truly excellent canalside pub. The map shows its location. Whilst on the walk, the high Downland provides many fine picnicking spots.

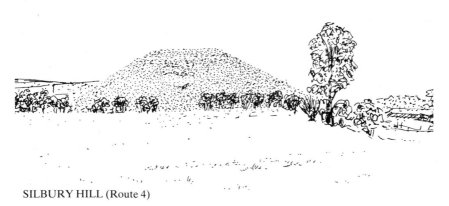

SILBURY HILL (Route 4)

Cherhill White Horse and Oldbury Castle

Outline   Cherhill ~ Oldbury Castle ~ Cherhill.

Summary   A stiff climb up to the ramparts of Oldbury Castle, over 800 feet above sea-level. Alongside this Iron Age fort lies one of the more famous of Wiltshire's chalk hill-figures, the Cherhill White Horse. Despite the lack of miles, the climb to the hilltop, the exploration of the fort and full enjoyment of the spectacular views will easily fill a good couple of hours. From Cherhill, it is only four miles to the village of Avebury with its famous stone circle.

Attractions   The Oldbury Hill-Fort, dating back to the Iron Age, covers some 20 acres. The site lies protected by a double bank and ditch, with a clear inturned entrance being visible on its eastern side. Youngsters will enjoy marching along the ramparts of the fort, and re-enacting past conflicts, whilst adults will probably prefer to relax and take in the far-ranging views of the surrounding Wiltshire countryside.

The Cherhill White Horse was cut in 1780 by a Doctor Christopher Alsop of nearby Calne. Nicknamed the 'mad doctor' because of his efforts in constructing this hill figure, his inspiration was probably the recently re-cut horse at Westbury. Tradition has it that the doctor stood one mile from the hillside with some sort of megaphone, shouting instructions to his men on the site who would mark out the figure's outline using white flags. The top turf could then be removed, and the cavity filled with chalk to form the figure. Rumour has it that when the local populace were opposing the construction of the Great Western Railway, many local coaching jobs depending upon the Great West Road that passes through Cherhill, Brunel - the GWR's engineer - was tempted to convert the white horse into a locomotive-shaped figure under cover of darkness! The nearby Landsdowne Monument of 1845, erected on the highest point along the Great West Road between London and Bath, commemorates the 17th century economist Sir William Petty. The Great West Road, now known less colourfully as just the A4, is much quieter today thanks to the opening of the M4 motorway.

The environment hereabouts is typical chalk downland, with soft cropped grass and the flora and fauna that are normally associated with the Downs. In high summer, with the sun beating down, the sky-lark singing high overhead and the delicate harebell blowing in the gentle breeze, this is English landscape at its best.   *continued on page 32*

Route 6

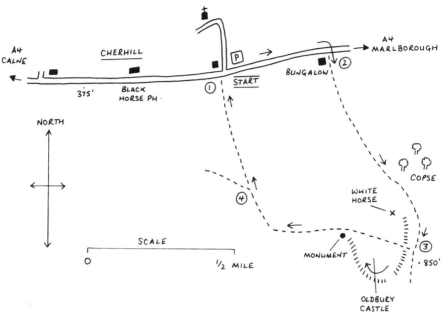

CHERHILL WHITE HORSE

Route 6

Cherhill White Horse and Oldbury Castle   2½ miles

START   *Cherhill village lies just off of the A4, some three miles east of Calne. Just past the lane that leads down to the village Church, there is a lay-by on the A4. Opposite, a rough track leading to the Downs is wide enough for sensible parking. (GR. 041701).*

ROUTE

1. *Follow the pavement alongside the A4 eastwards for about a quarter of a mile.*

2. *Just beyond a bungalow, follow the rough track on the right that heads off towards the White Horse. The track soon leads to a field path.*

3. *At the top of the hillside, follow the ramparts of the hill-fort returning eventually to the Landsdowne Monument. Follow the hill-top path westwards from the monument.*

4. *The hill-top path ends at a stile which is crossed to secure an enclosed chalk track. Follow the track straight down the hillside and back to the A4 at Cherhill.*

Public Transport   Occasional Bristol to London coaches that still use the A4 pass through Cherhill. Public transport is on the whole, however, poor in the area.

CHILDREN AT CHERHILL

Refreshments On the main A4 in Cherhill is the strangely named Black Horse Inn, offering snacks, meals and a garden. This Inn was once the base of the notorious Cherhill Gang who, stark naked, would terrorise the local neighbourhood during the hours of darkness! The full story and a painting of the gang in action can be seen inside the Inn. The Downland around the hill-fort makes a superb spot for picnicking.

BEECHES, OLIVER'S CASTLE

Oliver's Castle and Roundway Down, near Devizes

Outline   Roundway Down ~ Oliver's Castle ~ Roundway Down.

Summary   A short and very easy walk in an area north of Devizes where the Wessex Downs meet the clay vale of the Bristol Avon. The views in all directions are truly impressive, especially to the west from the ramparts of Oliver's Castle. This is one walk that even your youngest toddler could cope with, given time.

Attractions   The open downland that is crossed during the first half-a-mile of the walk is today just peaceful countryside with extensive views all around, but had you been walking here in 1643 then you would have soon been diving for cover. This is Roundway Down, scene all those years ago of a battle during the English Civil War. It was here that Sir William Waller and his Parliamentary troops were attacked by Royalist forces. Sir William fled the site, endowing it with the name 'Runaway' Hill - later to become the Roundway as it is know today.

As this is such a short walk, it provides an excellent opportunity to develop identification skills. The chalk soil supports a unique collection of flowers, ranging from the spotted orchid and the field scabious to the harebell and the chalk milkwort. A fascinating idea is to examine one square yard of the Downland, and to see how many different plants, flowers and grasses you can count. It may be possible, it will certainly prove a challenge, to spot as many as thirty different species. The unimproved chalk downland around Oliver's Castle is perhaps the richest area for flora. Attracted by all of the colourful plants and flowers are an array of butterflies. The meadow brown, the peacock, the red-admiral and the large white are especially common. Insects, too, are here in abundance - snails, aphids, slugs, ladybirds, bees and wasps. These in turn attract a varied number of birds, with the local arable crops providing a useful supplement to their diet. Finches, skylarks, pigeons, crows and even kestrels are found hereabouts. This is a whole community of living creatures, an ecosystem as the scientists call it, with total interdependence between the various species. An excellent book to bring with you on this walk is the Usborne Spotters Guide entitled 'Country Walks' which will soon have your youngster familiar with the more common species of birds, insects, flowers and grasses in the area.

Oliver's Castle is an enclosed site of 3½ acres protected by just a single rampart. The isolated beech trees dotted around this hilltop site

continued on page 36

33

Route 7

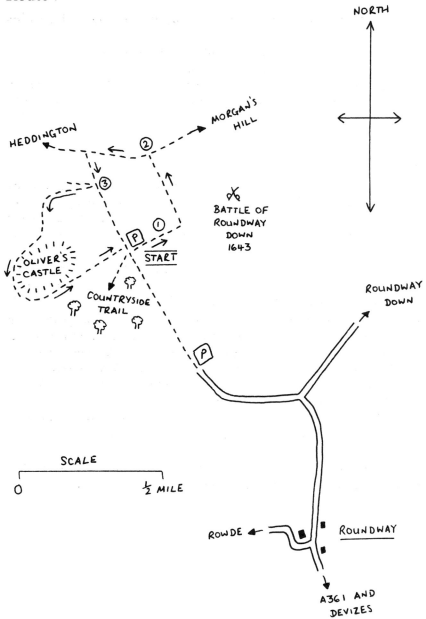

NORTH

MORGAN'S HILL

HEDDINGTON

② ③ ①

BATTLE OF ROUNDWAY DOWN 1643

START

OLIVER'S CASTLE

COUNTRYSIDE TRAIL

P

ROUNDWAY DOWN

SCALE

0   ½ MILE

ROWDE

ROUNDWAY

A361 AND DEVIZES

Route 7

Oliver's Castle and Roundway Down, near Devizes 1½ miles

START *One mile north-east of Devizes on the A361 road to Swindon, a left turn leads to the village of Roundway. A cul-de-sac lane is then followed up on to the Downs. Where the lane forks, bear left, and park either where the lane ends* (GR. 008641) *or drive a further half mile along the bumpy chalk track to Oliver's Castle, car suspension permitting* (GR. 005648).

ROUTE

1. *At the end of the chalk track, take the enclosed track on the right, which heads away from the escarpment. A few hundred yards along this track, bear left along another enclosed track. All the while, the paths are crossing the open tops of the downland, with fine views eastwards towards Tan Hill.*

2. *At a junction, turn left and follow a path that is enclosed on both sides by bushes and trees. After a few hundred yards, turn left through a gateway and follow another enclosed path across the top of the open downland.*

3. *Shortly, you reach a gateway on your right-hand side. Two paths leave from this entrance. The right-hand path heads downhill through a combe in the chalk escarpment. Our path is the left-hand one that follows the hilltop towards Oliver's Castle, clearly land-marked by the clumps of beech trees. Walk around the ramparts of the hillfort, before taking the obvious path back to the car-park.*

NB. *Adjacent to the parking area, a stile leads into some woodland. This is the start of the Roundway Hill Countryside Trail.*

Public Transport Badgerline operate a Bath to Salisbury service that passes through Devizes, two miles south of the start of the walk.

lend it a unique atmosphere, especially when noisy rooks and crows are circling around. The views from the western rampart are especially extensive, taking in the Avon Vale, Salisbury Plain and the distant Cotswold Hills. An ideal spot to pause and linger and enjoy a picnic.

Refreshments Devizes, an interesting old market town, lies just two miles from the walk. The town contains a good selection of pubs, cafes, and tea-shops. Devizes Museum houses many of the archaeological artifacts unearthed in this part of Curious Wessex. On the walk, the hilltop around Oliver's Castle makes a five-star picnic spot.

THE WESTBURY WHITE HORSE

Bratton and the Westbury White Horse

Outline Bratton ~ White Horse Farm ~ Bratton Camp ~ Bratton.

Summary Tracks and field-paths that embrace some of the most attractive downland in Southern England, together with Wiltshire's oldest white horse, an Iron Age hill-fort and a selection of stupendous views. An initial short, steep climb secures the high ground, with the bulk of the walk being along level paths high on the Downs. The last quarter of a mile back to Bratton involves a steep hillside descent.

Attractions England's chalk downland is under constant threat from the plough, with wheat being a more profitable commodity than lamb. Although much of the countryside covered by this walk is now arable land, significant amounts of the traditional downland remain. Throughout the year, an abundance of plants adorn the hillsides - cowslip, vetch, trefoil, milkwort and scabious being typical downland species - whilst the turf is kept cropped and springy by the constant nibbling of sheep and lambs. The hillsides around Combe Bottom, too steep for the plough, represent a perfect example of a traditional downland habitat. Dotted around the hill-tops are clumps of beech trees, so typical of the Wiltshire landscape.

Bratton Castle is an Iron Age hill-fort, with a double bank and ditch enclosing a site of some 25 acres. The views northwards from this commanding hilltop site are superb, ranging from the Mendips and the Cotswolds around to the Marlborough Downs and the Vale of Pewsey. A topograph on the hilltop provides detailed information about the town, villages and physical features it is possible to see. Within the fort is a long barrow, 230 feet long and 12 feet high.

The White Horse, close to the western rampart of the fort, was originally cut to commemorate Alfred's battle at Ethandun (nearby Edington?) in 878 AD., where the Danes were defeated. It was supposedly a 'squat ungainly creature with a reptilian tail' until in 1778 a Mr. Gee, steward of the local landowner Lord Abingdon, remodelled the horse to today's distinctive design. For his efforts he was labelled an 'ignorant destroyer'.

St. James Church, Bratton, a 13th century construction with a 15th century tower, is adorned with some particularly grisly-looking gargoyles, with one fine specimen adorning the north side of the nave. In

continued on page 40

Route 8

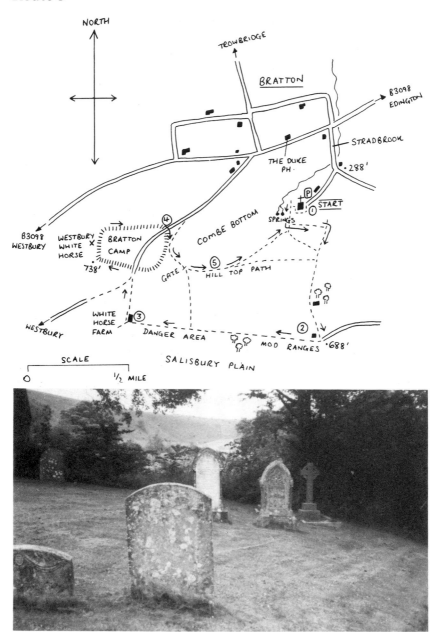

BRATTON CHURCHYARD

Route 8

Bratton and the Westbury White Horse   3½ miles

START   *Bratton lies on the B3098, some 3 miles east of Westbury. At the eastern end of the village, a turning on the right signposted 'Stradbrook - leading to Imber Road and Church Road' is taken. A short distance along Stradbrook, a right turn leads to St. James Church. There is ample parking by the Church. (GR. 914519).*

ROUTE

1. *Pass through the churchyard and on to a footpath at its western end. Turn left and follow this footpath up the hill as far as a stile on the left, cross this and continue through some wooded land to a track. Turn right and follow this track up steeply to a gate at the top. Continue across open countryside for over half-a-mile.*

2. *A barn marks the junction of our track with the lane that borders Salisbury Plain and the Imber Ranges. Turn right and continue along this lane until you reach White Horse Farm.*

3. *Turn right at White Horse Farm, and follow the track on to the southern ramparts of Bratton Camp. Follow the ramparts in a clockwise direction, passing the Westbury White Horse on your way.*

4. *When you reach the Bratton Road, cross it and continue on an unofficial path to a track down below the eastern ramparts of the Camp. Extensive views back towards Bratton open up on your left. Follow this track to a gate. Leave the more obvious path at this point and bear left to follow the hilltop path.*

5. *Keep to the left of the fence that borders the edge of the hilltop. Bratton Church lies down below at the end of Combe Bottom. Quarter of a mile along the hilltop path bear left down a steep field path which leads back to the Church.*

Public Transport   Badgerline operate a reasonably frequent service between Westbury and Devizes that passes through Bratton.

a hollow to the west of the Church lies a crystal-clear chalk stream, whose source can be traced clearly to the foot of the hillside. It is worth scrambling down the bank to find these Church Springs, not because Roman and Medieval coins and pottery have been found nearby but because these waters provide an excellent spot to cool hot and tired feet at the end of a fine downland walk!

Refreshments The Duke in Bratton offers meals, snacks and a garden. This would be an excellent place to eat and drink following a morning or an afternoon walking on the Downs. The Camp on the hilltop provides excellent picnicking spots, with ice-cream vans and, occasionally, a mobile fish-and-chip van, during summer weekends.

LOOKING NORTH FROM CLEY HILL

Route 9   4½ miles (or ½ mile)
Cley Hill near Warminster

Outline   A circular walk in the countryside around Cley Hill.

Summary   Flat field paths, country lanes and sunken tracks encircle Cley Hill, before the short, steep ascent of the knoll itself at the end of the walk. Families with very young children may simply prefer the walk to the top of Cley Hill (the ½ mile alternative).

Attractions   The 4 mile walk around the Cley Hill area enables this chalk knoll, some 750 feet in height, to be appreciated from all directions. Cley Hill, although no higher than the great chalk masses of the Wessex Downs and Salisbury Plain, appears more impressive because of its isolated setting amidst relatively flat agricultural land. Atop the hill are the remains of a Bronze Age hill-fort that encloses two obvious round barrows. The defensive potential of this site is clear, with open views extending towards the Mendips in the west, the Cotswolds to the north and Salisbury Plain and the Wessex Downs to the south and east. Immediately at hand to the south lies the finely wooded Longleat Estate.

In the late 1960s, Cley hill was a mecca for UFO hunters, with many alleged sitings from its summit on clear summer nights. Books with strange titles like 'UFOs over Warminster' appeared on the market, and hotels in this nearby town did a booming trade. The 'believers' explained these phenomena with reference to ley lines, several of which converge on Warminster, although cynics quickly pointed out that army exercises on nearby Salisbury Plain caused many lights in the night sky!

The circular walk around Cley Hill follows sunken paths, tracks and lanes through a rich agricultural countryside. The magnificent variety of flora that abound on the verges and in the hedgerows make this compulsory countryside for the owner of an 'I-Spy Wild Flowers' book. In early May, I spotted at least twenty different species of flora, including cowslip, wood anemone, common milkwort and the primrose.

Longleat, just a mile from Cley Hill, is well worth a visit. As well as the famous house and grounds, home of the Marquess of Bath, Europe's first Safari Park can be visited, where visitors can drive past hundreds of wild animals including the famous Longleat lions.

Refreshments   There are no public houses or cafes on this particular walk, although the town of Warminster some two miles away contains an abundance of such amenities.

Route 9

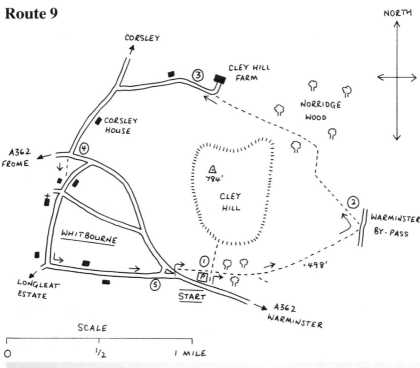

CORSLEY

CLEY HILL FARM
③

NORRIDGE WOOD

NORTH

CORSLEY HOUSE

A362 FROME ④

△ 784'

CLEY HILL

②
WARMINSTER BY-PASS

WHITBOURNE

498'

LONGLEAT ESTATE

①
P
START

⑤

A362 WARMINSTER

SCALE

0   ½   1 MILE

ROUND BARROW ON CLEY HILL

42

Route 9

Cley Hill near Warminster 4½ miles (or ½ mile)

START *Cley Hill lies just to the north of the A362 road between Warminster and Frome, some two miles west of Warminster. There is a car-park at the foot of the hill.* (GR. 838443).

ROUTE

1. *At the foot of Cley Hill, bear right along a sunken wooded track. This track emerges into open fields, and the right-hand hedgerow is followed to the Warminster by-pass.*
2. *Turn left and walk a short distance to the start of an enclosed track on the left. Follow this for ½ mile around the northern edge of Cley Hill. The track eventually becomes a field path that is followed downhill to a farm road.*
3. *Follow this farm road for ½ mile, and then turn left along a country lane.*
4. *Cross the A362 with care, pass through the kissing gate ahead, and head diagonally to the left-hand corner of the field ahead, to another kissing gate and a sunken country lane. Turn right and follow the road system as shown on the map to the A362.*
5. *Walk 20 yards along this busy and dangerous road, before crossing it to join a wooded track leading back to the foot of Cley Hill. End the walk with an ascent of the hill.*

Public Transport Badgerline operate a frequent Bath to Warminster service that passes close to Cley Hill.

STRIP LYNCHETTS, MIDDLE HILL

Route 10   5 miles

Scratchbury and Battlesbury Hills

Outline Bishopstrow ~ Battlesbury Hill ~ Middle Hill ~ Scratchbury Hill ~ Norton Bavant ~ Bishopstrow.

Summary A relatively long and energetic walk across three fine hills to the south-east of Warminster, two of which are capped with fine hill-forts. The views from the Downland hilltops are immense, although the price paid for this is one or two strenuous climbs that young inexperienced walkers may find quite demanding. The map indicates two 'escape' routes either side of Middle Hill that provide premature ways back to the busy A36 and Bishopstrow should the need arise. The final 1½ miles from the Heytesbury roundabout through Norton Bavant back to Bishopstrow is along flat field paths and lanes, with fine views to the east of the hills crossed earlier.

Attractions The track to the Downland ridge from Bishopstrow passes to the east of Battlesbury Hill and its Iron Age hill-fort, making a slight detour necessary if the actual site is to be visited. Dating from approximately 50BC, Battlesbury was probably a permanent settlement judging by the artefacts discovered in the vicinity -pottery, iron keys and saws, and parts of a chariot wheel. Rotary quern stones also indicated that corn was ground in the area. Middle Hill, although topped by a tumulus, was never the site of a hillfort. Its claim to fame are some fine strip lynchets on its eastern slopes. These man-made terraces were designed to ease cultivation on steep hillsides. Scratchbury Hill-Fort dates from the same era as Battlesbury, approximately 50BC. This double-banked fort with a ditch between, enclosed a huge area of some 37 acres. The banks and ditch will undoubtedly provide a fine spot for youngsters to engage in make-believe battles!

The open chalk downland around Scratchbury Hill is home to a rich variety of flora. In Spring and early Summer, cowslips, harebells, trefoil and common milkwort abound. It should also be possible to discover the occasional wild orchid. The views from Middle Hill and Scratchbury Hill are superb. To the east lie the military ranges on Salisbury Plain, no-go areas for walkers and ramblers. If exercises are in progress, you will see tanks and troop movements on the distant hillsides, as well as hearing the sound of gunshot. Ironically, military occupation of the Plain has prevented it disappearing under the plough, preserving its unique

continued on page 48

Route 10

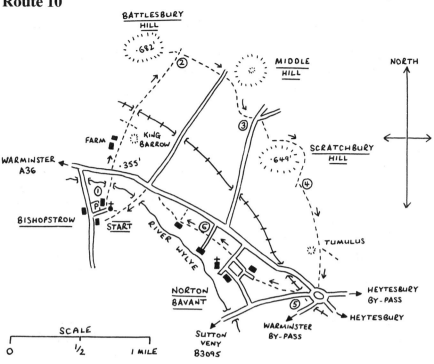

NORTH

BATTLESBURY
HILL

·682·

②

MIDDLE
HILL

③

FARM

KING
BARROW

SCRATCHBURY
HILL

·649·

④

WARMINSTER
A36

·355'

①

P

START

BISHOPSTROW

RIVER WYLYE

⑥

TUMULUS

NORTON
BAVANT

⑤

HEYTESBURY
BY-PASS

HEYTESBURY

WARMINSTER
BY-PASS

SUTTON
VENY
B3095

SCALE

0   ½   1 MILE

SPOTTED ORCHID

PINK/PURPLE

JUNE - AUGUST

Route 10

Scratchbury and Battlesbury Hills   5 miles

START   *From Warminster town-centre, take the A36 towards Salisbury. One mile out of Warminster, the B3095 forks off on the right towards Sutton Veny. Bishopstrow is just ½ a mile along the B3095, with the lane to the village Church on the left-hand side. There is ample parking on the lane near the Church. (GR. 895438).*

ROUTE

1. *Follow the path to the left-hand side of the Church, cross the River Wylye, and continue to the busy A36 road. Turn left, and 100 yards along the main road a track turns off on the right. Follow this track for 1 mile, passing a farm and a railway line, until you eventually reach the hilltop with Battlesbury Hill to your left.*

2. *Turn right, and head towards Middle Hill. The path across Middle Hill follows the southern edge of the hilltop, some 100 yards below the summit tumulus.*

3. *You eventually reach a lane below the eastern edge of Middle Hill. Opposite is a stile, beyond which lies the path that is followed around the northern and eastern ramparts of the hill-fort on Scratchbury Hill.*

4. *On the eastern side of Scratchbury Hill, cross the stile to your left and follow the path down the hillside to the A36 and Heytesbury roundabout.*

5. *Cross the roundabout, and its associated busy road complex, with care. Take the B3095 turning signposted to Sutton Veny. Immediately after the railway bridge, take the path on your right down into the field below. Follow the path across the fields to Norton Bavant, and pass through the village as shown on the map.*

6. *An obvious field path is taken towards Bishopstrow. Pass to the right of the house that 'blocks' the path midway between the two villages. At the far side of this house, cross the stile on your left which leads to another field path.*

7. *Where this field path meets the A36, turn left into Watery Lane. A hundred yards beyond the bridge that crosses the River Wylye, a stile on the right leads to a footpath that borders a stream. Follow this path back into Bishopstrow.*

Public Transport   Badgerline, in conjuction with the Wiltshire and Dorset Bus Company, operate a Swift Link service between Bristol and Salisbury that passes through Warminster and the villages along the A36 to the south of the town. Warminster Station lies just over 1 mile from the start of the walk.

Downland character. Below, beyond the A36, lies the River Wylye, with Cold Kitchen Hill (845 feet) prominent in the distance. To the north lies the isolated hillock of Cley Hill.

The return to Bishopstrow from the Heytesbury roundabout passes through the flat agricultural landscape that borders the River Wylye. Norton Bavant Church stands in a beautiful park, with its 14th century tower and turret, and a chalk arch. Within the Church, there are brasses of two husbands, John and Thomas Benet, and their wives, one with two groups of children. The footpath from Watery Lane to Bishopstrow passes a tributary stream of the Wylye, where hot feet can be cooled and refreshed, before the walk ends with a typical English scene - the village Church overlooking Bishopstrow's cricket green, with a fine oak tree at its side.

Refreshments   There are no public houses or cafes on this particular walk. Warminster, just over 1 mile from the end of the walk, contains many public houses and cafes. The hilltops on and around Scratchbury Hill provide many excellent picnicking spots.

STONEHENGE

Route 11

The Stonehenge Estate

Outline   A circular walk in the countryside around Stonehenge.

Summary   The area immediately around Stonehenge, with its car-park, tourists, security fences, souvenir and snack shops, and roped-off walkways, is really not very pleasant. This walk allows the ancient monument to be viewed from a distance, within its natural setting, far away from the hustle-and-bustle of the tourist traffic. The paths are all within National Trust land, and are generally level, clearly marked and well-defined. A number of important archaeological sites other than Stonehenge are included in this walk.

Attractions   Stonehenge is a prehistoric monument of worldwide fame, dating from 2800BC. Originally it was simply a henge monument consisting of a bank and external ditch. The concentric stone circles were a later addition. The stones are a mixture of sarsens from the nearby Marlborough Downs, and bluestones from the Prescelly Mountains in Wales. This was undoubtedly a sacred site for ancient man, although speculation as to its precise function continues to this day. A vast literature has been written on Stonehenge, and for a more-detailed treatment you should purchase one of the many booklets available at the site shop.

   To the south and east of Stonehenge lie two fine groups of barrows, those at Normanton Down, and the Old and New King Groups. The Normanton Down Barrows are arguably the finest collection in Britain, but their setting amongst fields of arable crops is disappointing. The New King Barrows, a collection of large round barrows, have a much more atmospheric location within a beech wood. The setting is cool, dark and shadowy, much more in keeping with the theme of ancient burial chambers.

   The Avenue would have provided a splendid approach to the Stonehenge site during ancient religious rituals. Today there is very little to see of this ceremonial walkway, although the National Trust information panel does say that aerial photography cleary shows a different coloured vegetation along the Avenue's route, the colouration being due to the man-made foundations that underlie its course.

   The Cursus is another site whose function remains a mystery. It is a remarkable enclosure consisting of two parallel banks and ditches, 100 yards apart and 1½ miles in length. Ploughing has destroyed much of the

continued on page 52

49

Route 11

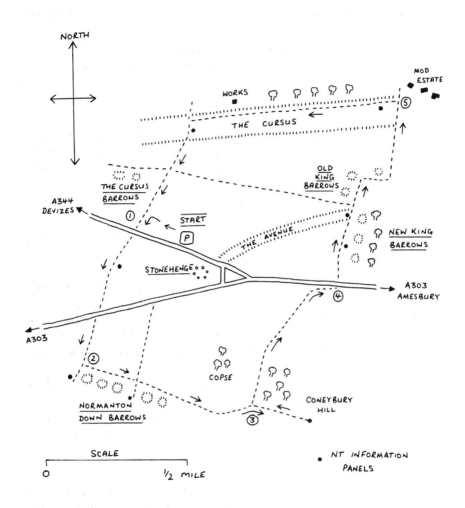

NORTH

MOD ESTATE

WORKS

THE CURSUS

⑤

OLD KING BARROWS

THE CURSUS BARROWS

A344 DEVIZES

①

START

P

NEW KING BARROWS

THE AVENUE

A303 AMESBURY

STONEHENGE

④

A303

②

COPSE

CONEYBURY HILL

NORMANTON DOWN BARROWS

③

SCALE

0   ½ MILE

• NT INFORMATION PANELS

Route 11

The Stonehenge Estate   4 miles

START   *Stonehenge lies just off the A303 trunk road, two miles west of Amesbury. There is a large car-park adjacent to the ancient monument. (GR. 123424).*

ROUTE

1. *Leave the car-park at its far end, through a gate by the area set aside for coaches. Turn left along a track, cross the A344, continue along the track ahead to the A303. Cross the A303, and continue along the clearly marked path towards the Normanton Down Barrows.*

2. *Take the stile on your left, and follow the field boundary for some distance. Direction signs clearly mark the route. Eventually the path drops into a small combe, and you climb the other side to arrive at the edge of a wood. The National Trust have clearly indicated the right of way with waymarker signs.*

3. *A short detour along the path on your right brings you to the summit of Coneybury Hill from where a fine view of the whole Stonehenge Estate can be obtained. Retracing your steps to the wood, turn right and follow the clearly marked path to the A303. Turn right, follow the footpath alongside this busy road for some 300 yards, where you cross the road and take the path alongside the New King Barrows.*

4. *Follow the clearly defined track, as shown on the map, past Old King Barrows and the eastern end of the Avenue.*

5. *At the eastern end of the Cursus, turn left. Follow the waymarked path along the course of the Cursus, to a track on the left. Follow the track back to the car-park.*

Public Transport   The Wiltshire and Dorset Bus Company operate a regular service between Salisbury and Stonehenge, connecting with Salisbury railway station.

site, although the banks and ditches are clearly visible at its western end. In view of the physical properties of the Cursus - its flatness, its width and its length - the suggestion that it was used for horse or chariot racing is perfectly feasible.

If all of this talk of ancient history becomes too much for youngsters, then the Stonehenge area can also offer a rich natural history. The very fortunate few might spot a roe deer. Hares are more common, whilst the sky-lark and the partridge both exist in large numbers. In the autumn months, large flocks of peewits will be seen feeding off the stubble and recently ploughed land. Salisbury Plain is also an area with a strong MOD presence. With the army base at Larkhill, and Boscombe Down Airfield, both within 3 miles of Stonehenge, many military vehicles and planes are likely to be seen on the roads and in the air around this ancient monument.

Refreshments   Drinks, light snacks and ice-creams are available at the Stonehenge site.

TRACK TO OLD SARUM

Route 12

3½ miles

Old Sarum

Outline   Old Sarum ~ Stratford-sub-Castle ~ the River Avon ~ Stratford-sub-Castle ~ Old Sarum.

Summary   Gentle walking, on the northern outskirts of Salisbury, based upon what was the original site of the city at Old Sarum. Suburbia is never far away, but the rural views, the River Avon and its neighbouring meadows easily outweigh the distractions of nearby semis and town buildings.

Attractions   Old Sarum is a site that has been occupied by just about every conceivable wave of settlers down through the ages. Iron Age settlers constructed the massive outer ramparts and ditches, and subsequently the Romans, the Saxons, the Danes and the Normans each in turn occupied the site and left their mark. In the 11th century the Normans built both a cathedral and a castle on this hilltop site. The soldiers proved such disagreeable neighbours for the clergy that in 1331 the cathedral was abandoned, and its materials moved to the site of New Sarum - modern Salisbury - where it was rebuilt. The outer ramparts and the ground plan of the cathedral are open freely at all times, whilst the remains of the castle within the inner ring can be viewed for a modest admission charge.

Below the hilltop site lies the River Avon and its bordering meadowland. The wide, shallow waters of this chalk stream are renowned for their dry fly fishing, and you will probably come across fishermen attempting to lure the local trout on to their hooks as you cross the river between Stratford-sub-Castle and Avon Farm. Where the Avon is crossed a second time, on the return to Stratford-sub-Castle, the waters are particularly accessible and, being clear and shallow, ideal for paddling. Remember to bring a towel because it is still one mile back to Old Sarum.

One landmark that you cannot miss on this walk is Salisbury Cathedral, just over one mile south of Old Sarum. The 404 foot spire is the highest in England, and completely dominates the city skyline. In the capstone of the spire is a tiny lead box with a fragment of woven fabric put there in 1375. It was supposedly a relic of the Virgin that would guard the spire from lightning and all harm. It is an interesting exercise to draw a straight line on the OS. map between Old Sarum and Salisbury Cathedral, and then to extend it to the north and south for several miles.

continued on page 56

Route 12

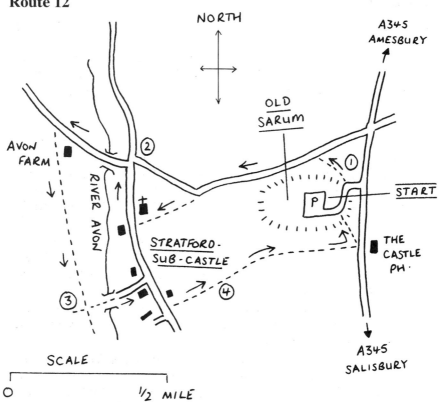

NORTH

A345 AMESBURY

OLD SARUM

AVON FARM

RIVER AVON

STRATFORD-SUB-CASTLE

START

P

THE CASTLE PH.

A345 SALISBURY

SCALE

0   1/2 MILE

VIEW TOWARDS SALISBURY

54

Route 12

Old Sarum   3½ miles

START   *Old Sarum lies a mile or so north of Salisbury on the A345 Amesbury road. Follow the signs into the ancient monument, where there is a large car-park inside the outer banks. (GR. 138327).*

ROUTE

1. *Follow the road back out of the car-park, and where it bears right to reach the main road turn left along the track that lies below the outer bank of Old Sarum. Turn left at the lane ahead. Where this lane bends to the right continue straight ahead along a sunken, tree-lined track to where it meets a road. Turn right passing St. Laurence's Church on the right.*

2. *Ignoring other possibilities, follow the road as it crosses the River Avon, and continue as far as a track on the left signposted to Avon Farm. Follow the track, then a footpath running parallel with the river for about a mile. At this point a metalled cross-path is reached.*

3. *Turn left, follow the path across the Avon and back into Stratford-sub-Castle. When you reach the road through the village, turn right in the general direction of Salisbury.*

4. *A few hundred yards along the road, look out for a path on the left that heads back to Old Sarum. It lies just this side of an estate road called St. Lawrence Close. Follow the obvious path back to the A345. You come out opposite the Castle public-house. A sign-post points the way back to Old Sarum.*

Public Transport   Old Sarum is on the northern outskirts of Salisbury, and is served by regular Wiltshire and Dorset buses from the city centre.

Northwards it passes through Stonehenge, whilst to the south it bisects Clearbury Ring, an Iron Age hillfort. This is a classic ley line. It really is an intriguing puzzle as to why so many ancient sites lie in straight lines. In between the sites, it is not uncommon to find marker stones, suggesting that ley lines were also ancient trackways.

Refreshments   The Castle, which lies on the A345 alongside Old Sarum, has a large garden, as well as offering meals and snacks. Adjacent to the car-park in Old Sarum is a large grassed area which is suitable for picnics, games of football and cricket, and generally running around to burn-off any excess energy.

GROVELY WOOD

Great Wishford and Grovely Wood

Outline   Great Wishford ~ Grovely Wood ~ Hadden Hill ~ Great Wishford.

Summary   A relaxing walk from the attractive village of Great Wishford, that lies in the Wylye valley between Warminster and Salisbury, up on to the wooded hills to the south-west, deep into the ancient forest of Grovely Wood. The paths are clear and distinct, and the gradients generally slight.

Attractions   Grovely Wood is an ancient forest that lies between the River Wylye to the north and east, and the River Nadder to the south. The best time to visit the wood is on May 29th, Oak Apple Day, when an ancient custom known as the Grovely Forest Rights is enacted. This annual ceremony is where the people of Great Wishford claim their right to collect 'all kinde of deade snappinge woode, boughes and stickes' from the local forest. Very early in the morning, the cry of 'Grovely, Grovely, Grovely and All Grovely' sounds forth, and the villagers proceed to the wood where an oak bough is cut. The bough is then decked in ribbons and carried ceremonially to Great Wishford Church where it is hung from the tower.

     The wood contains a large variety of trees, both deciduous and coniferous, and will speed youngsters on towards the Honourable Rank of Forester if they own a copy of the I-Spy Trees booklet. That monarch of trees, the oak, is found here in abundance, as are the ash, the beech and the hazel. With so many nut trees, a visit in early Autumn would be particularly profitable. Through the middle of the forest, where the path follows the course of an ancient Roman road from Salisbury to the West Country, there is a particularly impressive avenue of copper beech trees.

     As the path descends the downland back to Great Wishford, the views are far-ranging. In the combe to the left lies the road that was followed into the wood, ahead lies the Wylye valley, whilst beyond lies the massive chalk upland of Salisbury Plain. The valley carries the local transport links - the Bristol to Southampton railway and trunk road - as well as the River Wylye itself.

     Great Wishford Church is well worth a visit. It must be one of the only Churches to contain a fire engine, a red-and-black manual model dating from the 18th century and supposedly one of the oldest surviving

continued on page 60

57

Route 13

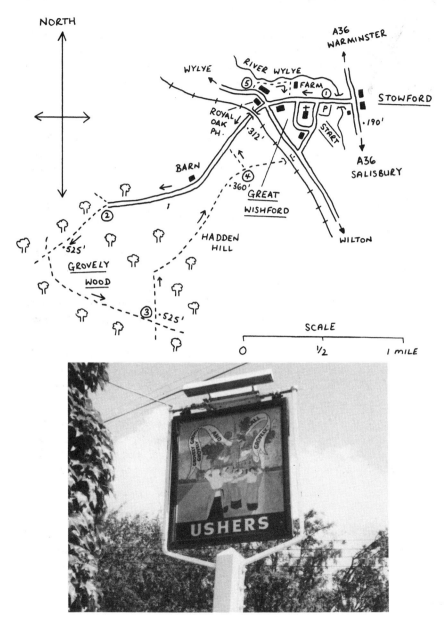

INN SIGN, GREAT WISHFORD

Route 13

Great Wishford and Grovely Wood   4 miles

START   *Great Wishford lies just off the A36 Salisbury to Warminster trunk road, three miles north of Wilton. As you enter the village, the Church of St. Giles is on your left-hand side. There is room for careful parking alongside the Church.* (GR. 080355).

ROUTE

1. *With the Church on your left-hand side, walk along the village street to the crossroads by the Royal Oak public-house. Cross straight over, pass under the railway bridge, and follow a quiet country lane along the foot of a combe for one mile.*

2. *The lane enters Grovely Wood, where it alternates between a flint track and a tarmac lane. Follow the lane for a further half-mile as it climbs steadily through Grovely Wood. At the top of the hill, turn left along the estate road. Follow this road for close on one mile through an avenue of copper beech trees.*

3. *A track crosses the estate road. Turn left, and follow this track out through the northern side of Grovely Wood. You eventually emerge on to open downland high on Hadden Hill. An enclosed path is followed down the hillside towards Great Wishford.*

4. *Either continue along this footpath back into the village or, better, take the obvious enclosed path on the left just before entering the village. When you reach the lane turn right and follow it back to the Royal Oak. Continue to the start.*

5. *(An optional detour) Turn left at the Royal Oak, and follow the road until you pass the last house on the right-hand side. Take the next gateway on the right down to the river-bank. Follow the river-bank to the farm buildings ahead, where you take the lane to the right back to the village Church.*

Public Transport Badgerline and the Wiltshire and Dorset Bus Company operate a Swift Link service between Bristol, Bath and Salisbury that passes Stoford Bridge, just 400 yards from the start of the walk.

manual fire-engines. On the outside of the eastern boundary wall of the Church are the breadstones, engraved stones that record the price of a gallon of bread at various times since 1800. Then the humble loaf was 3/4 (17p) a gallon. By 1984 it was £1.80 - such is inflation! The Church contains a memorial to a Sir Thomas Bonham who was so upset when his wife gave birth to twins that he reputedly disappeared to the Holy Land on a crusade for seven years. Upon his return his wife allegedly rewarded him with septuplets who were carried to the Church in a sieve to be Christened. A brass commemorates Sir Thomas and the nine children, although the sieve has long since disappeared from the Church.

Refreshments   In the village of Great Wishford is the Royal Oak that serves bar-snacks. There are also outdoor tables where youngsters could be accomodated. On the walk itself, the enclosed path back to Great Wishford from Grovely Wood, high on Hadden Hill, would be an excellent place for a picnic.

FOVANT BADGES

The Fovant Badges

Outline   Fovant ~ Fovant Badges ~ Chiselbury Camp ~ Fovant.

Summary   Wiltshire is renowned for her chalk hill-figures, and this walk is centred upon an unusual group of military badges carved on the downland escarpment above Fovant. Fovant lies in the south of the county, a few miles west of Salisbury, but the landscape is a familiar one of chalk downs and clay vale. The walk itself is short, with the climb on to the downland hilltop being its only strenuous feature.

Attractions   The Fovant Badges are carved on the steep north-western slopes of Fovant Down. During the First World War, many troops were billeted at training camps in the locality before seeing action on the Western Front. Early each morning, volunteers would work on the emblems, with each design taking several months to complete. The London Rifle Brigade thought up the idea of the Badges, and theirs was the first to be cut. The other badges include those of the Royal Wiltshire Yeomanry, the Sixth London Rifles and the Royal Warwickshire Yeomanry. The collection is certainly impressive, and many a motorist on the A30 must have been distracted from the road ahead by this most unusual site.

On the hilltop above the badges lies the remains of a much earlier military occupation, Chiselbury Camp. This is an Iron Age hill-fort dating from about 200BC, consisting of a single bank, with double ramparts on the vulnerable south-western side. The enclosure extends to some nine acres. At over 650 feet above sea-level, and sited atop a steep escarpment, the camp provides an excellent viewpoint overlooking Fovant and the Nadder Valley below. Given the commanding views from the site, and the protection afforded by the steep hillside slope, it is obvious why this site was chosen for such a settlement.

Refreshments   At the start of the walk are two public-houses, the Pembroke Arms and the Cross Keys, that offer everything from accomodation and breakfast to souvenirs and cider! One mile out of Fovant, on the road to Wilton, is the Emblems Cafe, where in addition to good food there is a fine view of the Fovant Badges.

Route 14

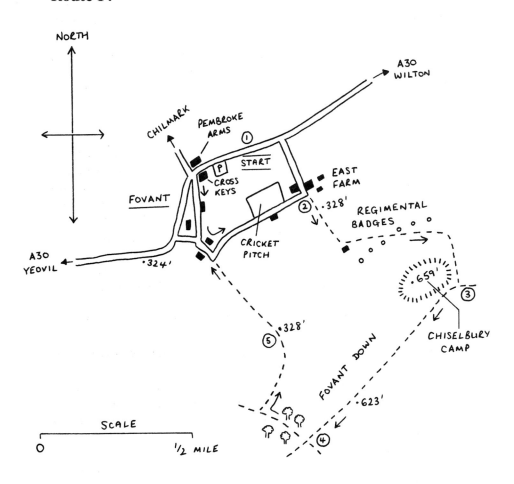

NORTH

A30 WILTON

CHILMARK

PEMBROKE ARMS

① START

P

CROSS KEYS

FOVANT

EAST FARM

② •328'

REGIMENTAL BADGES

•659'

③

CHISELBURY CAMP

A30 YEOVIL

•324'

CRICKET PITCH

⑤ •328'

FOVANT DOWN

•623'

④

SCALE

0   ½ MILE

62

Route 14

The Fovant Badges   2 miles

START   *Fovant lies six miles west of Wilton on the A30 trunk road between Salisbury and Yeovil. As you enter the village from Wilton, just before the Cross Keys public house there is a lay-by with room for several cars. (GR. 007286).*

ROUTE

1. *Walk carefully along the A30 to the Cross Keys, and take the lane to the left immediately past the inn. Follow the lane to a junction where you bear left. At the end of a group of houses, a stile faces you. Ignore this option, instead turning left and taking the lane that leads towards East Farm. The Fovant Badges can be seen on the hillside to your right.*

2. *At the farm, the lane turns to the left. Our path is across the gate and into the field on the right-hand side. Continue straight ahead, towards the badges, keeping the field boundary to your right. At the far side of the field, look for the path on your left-hand side that climbs diagonally up the scarp slope of the hillside. At the top, the banks of Chiselbury hill-fort lie directly ahead. Follow the eastern bank out on to a bridlepath.*

3. *Turn right, and follow the bridlepath along the hilltop for just over half a mile, to a crossroads of paths.*

4. *Turn right and begin the descent of the hillside. For quarter of a mile the path passes through bushes and woodland before emerging on to the downland escarpment. Continue on until you meet a path coming up from the right that cuts diagonally across the hillside. Follow this path to the foot of the hill where a stile is reached.*

5. *Cross the stile into a field and, keeping the boundary fence to your left, head back towards Fovant. You reach the stile ignored in direction 1. Retrace your steps to your vehicle.*

FIELD-PATH FROM COLD KITCHEN HILL

The Deverills and Cold Kitchen Hill

Outline   Kingston Deverill ~ Cold Kitchen Hill ~ Brixton Deverill ~ The River Wylye ~ Kingston Deverill.

Summary   A fine walk in and around the group of villages to the south of Warminster known as the Deverills. From Kingston Deverill, there is a stiff climb of some 400 feet up to the summit of Cold Kitchen Hill, from where far-ranging views of this part of south and west Wiltshire can be obtained. The path drops down to Brixton Deverill, where the banks of the River Wylye are followed back to Kingston Deverill.

Attractions   The Deverills are a group of five villages lying along a wide vale between fine chalk hills, some four or five miles south of Warminster. From north to south, Longbridge Deverill, Hill Deverill, Brixton Deverill, Monkton Deverill and Kingston Deverill lie no more than four miles apart along the road from Warminster to Mere. The word Deverill can be interpreted 'the river of the fertile upland region', the river in question being the Wylye which flows through all five villages.
     Cold Kitchen implies meatless bones, and could have associations with an extensive Romano-Celtic temple and cremation area, the site of which lies on the hillside to the north-west of the triangulation pillar. Many partially burnt Romano-Celtic brooches were found during excavations of the temple site, indicating the presence of a crematorium, with nearby Brimsdown Hill being further substantiating evidence, Brimsdown being a name associated with fire. From Cold Kitchen Hill, the views range far in all directions. Cley Hill is visible to the north, Warminster to the north-east, Cow Down to the east, the Deverills lie below in the valley, and the isolated chalk hills of Long Knoll and Little Knoll lie to the west.
     The long barrow just below the triangulation pillar is 230 feet long and 8 feet in height. Referred to as 'lang beorh' in a Saxon charter, this particular barrow has prominent side ditches, and dates back to 3000 or 4000BC. Another common feature of the Downland landscape can be seen close to where the hilltop path meets the chalk track that leads down to Brixton Deverill. An isolated depression in the ground is in fact a dew-pond. Chalk, being porous, will not retain water. On hilltop sites, ponds were dug and lined with clay, to retain water and act as reservoirs for the upland settlements.   *continued on page 68*

Route 15

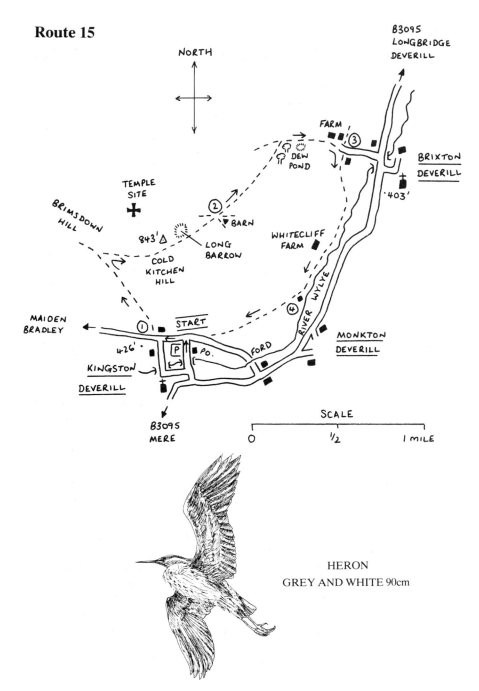

NORTH

B3095
LONGBRIDGE
DEVERILL

FARM

③

BRIXTON
DEVERILL

TEMPLE
SITE

DEW
POND

'403'

BRIMSDOWN
HILL

②

BARN

843' △

LONG
BARROW

WHITECLIFF
FARM

COLD
KITCHEN
HILL

RIVER WYLYE

④

MAIDEN
BRADLEY

①

START

MONKTON
DEVERILL

426'

P

P.O.

FORD

KINGSTON

DEVERILL

B3095
MERE

SCALE

0

½

1 MILE

HERON
GREY AND WHITE 90cm

66

Route 15

The Deverills and Cold Kitchen Hill   4 miles

START   *From Warminster, follow the A350 Shaftesbury road for two or three miles to Longbridge Deverill. Turn right along the B3095 Mere road, and it is just three miles to Kingston Deverill. On the edge of Kingston Deverill, turn right along a lane signposted to Maiden Bradley. Pass the village Post Office on the right, beyond which there is ample parking space on the left-hand side. (GR. 846373).*

ROUTE

1. *Follow the lane out of the village as shown on the map. Just beyond the last house on the right-hand side, cross the stile and take the obvious path that climbs to the hilltop. Follow the hilltop fence to the right, and soon a clear path will be visible directly ahead that leads to the distant triangulation pillar at the summit of Cold Kitchen Hill. Continue on past the pillar downhill to a barn, with the long barrow on your left-hand side.*

2. *Ignore the obvious chalk track that leads downhill immediately ahead. Instead, pass into the fields on your left-hand side. Follow the boundary fence on towards some trees, where you join a track. Bear right and follow the track downhill to Brixton Deverill. On the very edge of the village, you pass a farm on your left-hand side.*

3. *Just past the farm, turn right along a path immediately before a thatched cottage. The path actually appears to lead into the garage alongside the cottage! Beyond the cottage, the right of way passes through a paddock, with the River Wylye just a few yards away on your left-hand side. Secure the river bank, which is followed across several fields to the front of Whitecliff Farm. Cross the driveway in front of the farm, and continue on along the river bank until you reach a group of buildings and the end of the accessible river bank.*

4. *Take the gateway on the right-hand side and follow the path up the hillside to a gate. Pass through the gate, and continue on along the hillside path, with the field boundary on your left-hand side. The field paths eventually bring you to a hedgerow and a country lane, where you turn right for the short walk back to Kingston Deverill. If you have any energy left, a short detour to the left when you reach the lane will bring you to a ford through the River Wylye, as marked on the map.*

Public Transport   The Deverills are not served by a reliable and frequent bus service.

The path back to Kingston Deverill from Brixton Deverill follows a section of the River Wylye. Hereabouts, we are near the source of this chalk stream which flows north-eastwards to Warminster, before turning south-eastwards to join the River Nadder at Wilton. The waters are clear, shallow and accessible, perfect for paddling. The birdlife along the river bank is rich and varied. This is due to a mixture of habitats within the immediate area. As well as the river, there are trees, scrubland and hillside slopes, each of which attracts different species of birds. If you are fortunate, you could well spot a sparrowhawk or a kestrel, or mallard or a kingfisher, a greater spotted woodpecker or even a heron. These are all in addition to the more common species like the yellow-hammer, the goldfinch and the carrion crow. A good pair of binoculars are especially useful.

Refreshments There are public houses in Maiden Bradley and in Longbridge Deverill, where the George would be inviting, following a vigorous morning's or afternoon's walking. The river bank alongside the Wylye would be an excellent spot for a picnic.

PATH TO WHITE SHEET HILL

Route 16

Stourhead and White Sheet Hill

Outline Stourton ~ White Sheet Hill ~ The Stourhead Estate ~ Stourton.

Summary A circular walk that links two of the National Trust's properties in south-west Wiltshire - the Stourhead Estate, with its house and gardens, and the nearby White Sheet Hill, an area of unimproved chalk downland that is home to a number of archaeological sites. The generally flat lanes, tracks and paths make for easy going, with just the one climb on to White Sheet Hill to contend with. At the end of the walk, you will want to allow yourself two or three hours to visit the varied attractions of the Stourhead Estate, including the Spreadeagle Inn!

Attractions The village of Stourton is soon left behind, and you will be striding out along the lane that leads to Search Farm. Wide views gradually open up all around - the Blackmoor Vale with the Dorset Downs beyond lie to the south, Long Knoll, Little Knoll and Cold Kitchen Hill lie to the north, and the imposing White Sheet Hill lies directly ahead. As the route climbs White Sheet Hill, the views become even more widespread, and it is possible to look back towards Stourton and beyond to Alfred's Tower, high on the wooded land that forms the Wiltshire - Somerset border.

White Sheet Hill, as well as being a fine viewpoint, is an archaelogist's dream. At the southern end is a hill-fort, protected by a single bank and ditch on the steepest sides and three banks and ditches on the flatter north-eastern side. Across the middle of the hilltop runs a cross-ridge dyke, probably associated with the Iron Age hill-fort, the function of which was to control the movement of livestock. At the northern end of the hill lies the site of a causewayed enclosure dating from 3000BC. The hilltop is now National Trust property, and is maintained as unimproved chalk grassland, where the plough and fertiliser are banned. The result is an abundance of flora, including the cowslip, orchids, vetches and campanulas, as well as butterflies, including the rare chalkhill blue. As a concession to modern times, the hilltop is used by the local Model Aircraft Club, and at weekends it is normal to find twenty or thirty enthusiasts flying their varied craft high above the downs. Around the hilltop, the track that forms our route back to the Red Lion Inn is an ancient route from Salisbury to the West Country. Alongside the track, a milestone erected in 1752, records that we are 'XX111 miles from Sarum'.

continued on page 72

Route 16

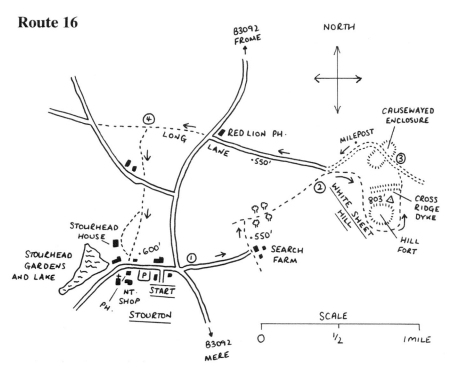

NORTH

B3092 FROME

CAUSEWAYED ENCLOSURE

④ LONG LANE

RED LION PH.

·550'

MILEPOST

③

②

WHITE SHEET HILL

803' △

CROSS RIDGE DYKE

HILL FORT

STOURHEAD HOUSE

STOURHEAD GARDENS AND LAKE

·600'

①

·550'

SEARCH FARM

NT. SHOP

PH.

START

STOURTON

B3092 MERE

SCALE

0   ½   1 MILE

A REAL TURNSTILE, STOURHEAD

70

Route 16
Stourhead and White Sheet Hill   4 miles

START   *Stourton village, Stourhead House and Stourhead Gardens lie just off of the B3092 Frome to Mere road, about ten miles south of Frome. With Stourhead being one of the National Trust's most famous properties, the location is well signposted for several miles around. Just after turning off the B3092, there is a large National Trust car-park on the left-hand side. (GR. 778341).*

ROUTE

1. *Walk back to the B3092, and almost opposite is a lane which is followed for half a mile to Search Farm. At the farm, bear left along the bridleway, cross the gate immediately ahead and follow the fieldpath on to another track. At the track, turn right and continue on towards White Sheet Hill, passing through a beech copse on your way.*

2. *At the top of the chalk escarpment, cross the stile to your right and follow the hillside fence to the top of White Sheet Hill. The hilltop is National Trust property with free access rights, meaning that there are no specific pathways. Our walk follows the hilltop to the south, encircles the hill-fort and its ramparts, passes back to the triangulation pillar, and then joins a chalk track by the NT. information board.*

3. *Follow the chalk track around the back of the hilltop, and then down the hill in the direction of Stourhead. Shortly, the track becomes a country lane which is followed for half a mile to the Red Lion Inn and the B3092. Cross the B3092, and follow the enclosed grass track immediately opposite.*

4. *After almost half a mile following this enclosed, sunken pathway, look out for a stile at the top of the bank to your left. Head directly south from this stile, following the field boundaries at first, until you emerge on a country lane just to the left of the dwellings that lie ahead. Immediately opposite is a gateway that takes you into the Stourhead estate and on to an obvious path back to the village of Stourton.*

Beyond the Red Lion Inn, the track becomes sunken and hedged-in, with two stately trees - the ash and the oak - dominating the hedgerows. Their presence reminds me of an old rhyme, used by our forefathers to make long-range weather forecasts:

Oak before ash, we're in for a splash,
Ash before oak, we're in for a soak.

Whichever tree burst into leaf first would give some indication of that summer's rainfall, a splash meaning light showers, with a soak indicating a wet summer!

The final half-mile of the walk bring us to the Stourhead Estate. Henry Hoare, a wealthy London banker, bought the manor of Stourton in 1718, demolished the old Stourton House and in its place erected an imposing Palladian mansion, Stourhead House. The House contains a fine collection of art treasures and furniture, some of which was made by Thomas Chippendale on the premises. From the footpath, a fine view of the frontage of Stourhead House is obtained. The road outside of the entrance gate to the House leads down to the village of Stourton and Stourhead Gardens, one of the most famous landscaped gardens in the world. What was once a series of medieval fishponds was transformed in the 18th century by Henry Hoare's son, (another Henry) into one of the earliest idyllic landscapes in England. A lake is the central focus, surrounded by classical temples, bridges and rustic grottos, rare specimens of trees and plants, and a steady succession of flowers that add beauty throughout the seasons. Snow drops are followed by daffodils and bluebells, which in turn are followed by rhododendrons, camellias, magnolias and azaleas. The Hoare Family gave the Stourhead Estate to the National Trust in 1946, since when its character and atmosphere have been carefully maintained.

Refreshments   On the return from White Sheet Hill, you pass the Red Lion Inn on the B3092. This hostelry serves snacks, lunches and real ale, as well as offering bed-and-breakfast and a garden. In the village of Stourton, there is the Spreadeagle Inn as well as the refreshment facilities offered by the National Trust. The open land on White Sheet Hill is suitable for picnicking.

Appendices

APPENDIX 1 — mileages for motorists.

The chart below shows the approximate distance in miles between certain towns within Wiltshire. The City of Bath has also been included, being just a few miles from the Wiltshire boundary. Motoring within Wiltshire poses few problems. The county is criss-crossed by several major roads, chiefly those between London and the West Country, and the Midlands and Southampton, which means that fairly substantial distances can be covered in very reasonable times. My own experience illustrates this. I live in Bradford-on-Avon in the extreme west of the county, and yet all of the walks are within an hour's drive of my home. Many are in fact much closer.

	BATH	CHIPPENHAM	MALMESBURY	MARLBOROUGH	PEWSEY	SALISBURY	SWINDON	TROWBRIDGE	WARMINSTER
BATH	—	12	22	31	34	40	31	11	19
CHIPPENHAM	12	—	10	19	25	35	19	13	20
MALMESBURY	22	10	—	22	28	46	15	23	30
MARLBOROUGH	31	19	22	—	6	28	12	25	32
PEWSEY	34	25	28	6	—	21	19	24	27
SALISBURY	40	35	46	28	21	—	40	31	21
SWINDON	31	19	15	12	19	40	—	30	34
TROWBRIDGE	11	13	23	25	24	31	30	—	9
WARMINSTER	19	20	30	32	27	21	34	9	—

APPENDIX 2 — Wet Weather Alternatives. Completely or partly under cover.

Museums and Art Galleries

Devizes Museum, Long Street, Devizes. Open all year. Tuesday to Saturday. Excellent displays of local archaeology and natural history.

Duke of Edinburgh's Royal Regiment Museum, Cathedral Close, Salisbury. Open Sunday to Friday, April to September; and Monday to Friday, October to March.

Dewey Museum, Warminster Library, Three Horseshoes Mall, Warminster. Open all year round, excluding Sundays and Wednesdays. Local history, archaeology and geology.

Great Barn Museum of Wiltshire Folk Life, Avebury. Open daily April to October, and some winter weekends.

Richard Jefferies Museum, Coate Water, Swindon. Open Wednesday, Saturday and Sunday, afternoon only. A tribute to the well-known writer (see walk 1).

Alexander Keiller Museum, Avebury. Open daily throught the year. Displays of the Neolithic monuments of the Avebury complex.

Salisbury and South Wiltshire Museum, Cathedral Close, Salisbury. Open Monday to Saturday throughout the year, and on Sundays in July and August. Many beautifully designed galleries, including displays on Stonehenge and Old Sarum.

Swindon Museum and Art Gallery, Bath Road, Swindon. Open daily throughout the year.

Yelde Hall Museum, Market Place, Chippenham. Open Monday to Saturday, March to October. Housed in a late 15th century building; contains items of local historical interest.

Trowbridge Museum, Civic Hall, Trowbridge. Open Tuesday and Saturday mornings throughout the year. Historical displays on the town and its locality.

Athelstan Museum, Town Hall, Malmesbury. Open Tuesday to Saturday, April to September, and Wednesday, Friday and Saturday, October to March. Displays of local history and archaeology.

Fox Talbot Museum of Photography, Lacock, Chippenham. Open daily, March to October.

Industrial Interest

Bedwyn Stone Museum, Great Bedwyn near Marlborough. Open daily throughout the year.

Crofton Pumping Station, Kennet and Avon Canal, Crofton near Marlborough. Open Sundays, April to October.

Great Western Railway Museum, Faringdon Road, Swindon. Open daily throughout the year.

Kennet and Avon Canal Exhibiton, The Wharf, Devizes. Open daily Easter to October.

Railway Village Museum, 34 Faringdon Road, Swindon. Open daily throughout the year.

Wilton Windmill, Wilton, Marlborough. Open Sundays and Bank Holidays, Easter to September.

Historic Buildings.

Avebury Manor, Avebury. Open April to October daily, and November to March, Tuesday, Thursday and weekends.

Bowood House and Gardens, Calne. Open daily April to September.

Chalcot House, near Westbury. Open daily during July and August.

Corsham Court, Corsham. Open daily mid-January to mid-December, except Mondays and Fridays.

Lacock Abbey and Grounds. Open daily April to October.

Longleat House and Grounds, near Warminster. Open daily throughout the year.

Lydiard Mansion, Purton, near Swindon. Open daily throughout the year.

Mompesson House, Salisbury. Open April to October, excluding Thursdays and Fridays.

Sheldon Manor, Chippenham. Open April to October, Sundays, Thursdays and Bank Holidays.

Stourhead House and Gardens, near Mere. House open April to October, Saturday to Wednesday. Gardens open daily throughout the year.

New Wardour Castle, Tisbury. Open school summer holidays, Monday, Wednesday, Friday and Saturday.

Wilton House, Wilton, Salisbury. Open Easter to October, Tuesday to Saturday.

Malmesbury Abbey, Malmesbury. Open daily throughout the year.

Salisbury Cathedral, Salisbury. Open daily throughout the year.

APPENDIX 3 — Some other places of interest.

Wessex Shire Park, Teffont Magma, Salisbury. 130 acres of activities related to traditional farming and countryside pursuits.
Link Centre Ice Rink, Swindon.
Oasis Centre, Swindon. Lagoon pool, wave machine, hydro-slide and water chutes.
Brokerswood Woodland Park, near Trowbridge. Woodland heritage centre. Open daily throughout the year.
Longleat Safari Park, near Warminster. Open daily March to October.

A selection of trails.

Arn Hill, Warminster. 2 mile circular walk through woodland, scrubland and open downland. Open all year.
Blackland Lakes Nature Trail, Calne. Open daily Easter to October.
Clouts Wood, near Wroughton. 1½ miles through ancient woodland. Interesting flowers. Open all year.
Lydiard Country Park Nature Trail, near Swindon. 1½ miles through country park. Open all year.
Mortimore's Wood, Chippenham. Nature trail with many varieties of woodland and aquatic life. Open all year.
Postern Hill Walk, near Marlborough. Trail through beech and oak woods in ancient forest. Roe and fallow deer. Open all year.
Roundway Hill Countryside Trail, near Devizes. One mile trail around Roundway Hill. Open all year.
Scotchel Nature Trail, Pewsey. Unusual plants, wildlife and trees. Open all year.
To fully appreciate a particular trail, contact the nearest Tourist Information Centre for informative literature. Their addresses are contained in Appendix 5.

APPENDIX 4 — Bus Operators in the Wiltshire Area.

Badgerline .... Tel. Bath 64446
Thamesdown Transport .... Tel. Swindon 23700
Wilts and Dorset .... Tel. Salisbury 336855

APPENDIX 5 — Tourist Information Centres within the area.

Amesbury	Redworth House, Flower Lane	Tel. Amesbury (0980) 22833
Avebury	The Great Barn	Tel. Avebury (06723) 425
Bath	Abbey Churchyard	Tel. Bath 62831
Bradford on Avon	34 Silver Street	Tel. B-on-A (02216) 2495
Calne	Lansdowne Strand Hotel	Tel. Calne (0249) 812488
Chippenham	The Neeld Hall, High Street	Tel. Chippenham (0249) 657733
Corsham	Methuen Arms Hotel	Tel. Corsham (0249) 714867
Devizes	The Canal Centre, The Wharf	Tel. Devizes (0380) 71069
Malmesbury	Town Hall	Tel. Malmesbury (06662) 2143
Marlborough	St. Peter's Church, High St.	Tel. Marlborough (0672) 53989
Melksham	Roundhouse, Church Street	Tel. Melksham (0225) 707424
Mere	The Square	Tel. Mere (0747) 860341
Salisbury	Malthouse Lane	Tel. Salisbury (0722) 334956
Swindon	32, The Arcade, Brunel Centre	Tel. Swindon (0793) 30328
Warminster	The Library	Tel. Warminster (00985) 218548
Westbury	The Library Car Park	Tel. Westbury (0373) 827158

Other Useful Addresses.

> **The National Trust,** Regional Information Office, Stourton, Warminster. Tel. Bourton (Dorset) (0747) 840224.
>
> **Wilts County Council,** Press and Public Relations Office, Wilts County Council, County Hall, Trowbridge. Tel. Trowbridge (02214) 3641.
>
> **West Country Tourist Board,** Trinity Court, Southernhay East, Exeter. Tel. Exeter (0392) 76351.

NB. All telephone codes are from **Outside** the locality. Within the area, there are local dialling codes.

APPENDIX 6 — Routes in Order of Difficulty.

As an experienced walker, I would class all of the walks in this book as easy if I were tackling them on my own. However, these are Family Walks and the grading should be read with this in mind. They apply to a fairly active six or seven year old, rather than a hardened veteran!

Easy Walks:

    Route 1 - *Barbury Castle.*
    Route 6 - *Cherhill White Horse and Oldbury Castle.*
    Route 7 - *Oliver's Castle and Roundway Down.*
    Route 12 - *Old Sarum.*
    Route 13 - *Great Wishford and Grovely Wood.*
    Route 14 - *The Fovant Badges.*

Moderately Difficult:

    Route 2 - *Fyfield Down and the Sarsen Stones.*
    Route 3 - *Woodborough, Wilcot and the Kennet and Avon Canal.*
    Route 4 - *Avebury, Silbury Hill and the Ridgeway.*
    Route 5 - *The Pewsey Down Nature Reserve and the Wansdyke.*
    Route 9 - *Cley Hill near Warminster.*
    Route 11 - *The Stonehenge Estate.*

More Strenuous:

    Route 8 - *Bratton and the Westbury White Horse.*
    Route 10 - *Scratchbury and Battlesbury Hills.*
    Route 15 - *The Deverills and Cold Kitchen Hill.*
    Route 16 - *Stourhead and White Sheet Hill.*

THE FAMILY WALKS SERIES

General Editor: Norman Taylor

Family Walks in the White Peak.
Norman Taylor. Published 1985. Reprinted 1985. Revised edition 1987.
Described in The Great Outdoors as "quite simply, the best Peak District short walks guide yet published."

Family Walks in the Dark Peak. Norman Taylor. 1986.

Family Walks in the Cotswolds. Gordon Ottewell. 1986.

Family Walks around Bristol, Bath and the Mendips. Nigel Vile. 1987.

Family Walks in Hereford and Worcester. Gordon Ottewell. 1988.

Family Walks in the Downs and Vales of Wiltshire. Nigel Vile. 1988.

IN PREPARATION
Family Walks in South Yorkshire
Family Walks in the Wye Valley
Family Walks around Newbury
Family Walks in North Gwent

The Publishers, D. J. Mitchell and E. G. Power welcome suggestions for further titles in this Series and will be pleased to hear from suitably experienced walkers.

FORTHCOMING
The Pennine Way Pub Guide. Chris Harrison. Autumn 1988.
Covers every pub within one mile of the Pennine Way, with notes on beer, food, accommodation, and glimpses of the building's history and oral tradition. Maps and photographs.

SOME OTHER SCARTHIN BOOKS

Journey from Darkness. Gordon Ottewell. £2.25
An adventure story for 9-12 year olds, following the hazardous journey of two pit-boys and a pony through the Derbyshire countryside of Victorian days. Described by one young reader as "Brill!"

Our Village: Alison Uttley's Cromford. Alison Uttley. £2.85
Published for the Alison Uttley Centenary in 1984 and reprinted with an introduction by Denis Judd in 1987. A selection of her essays describe the Country Child's girlhood in Victorian Cromford. Illustrations by C. F. Tunnicliffe from the original editions.

First Loves: Life Stories of Victorian Dolls. Lilian McCrea. £5.95
Large format hardback, with colour photographs of the dolls themselves from the author's collection. Lilian McCrea retells the stories, amusing and sad, which she heard from the original owners.

FORTHCOMING
Country of Stone Walls. Helen Perkins.
D. H. Lawrence's associations with the Peak District of Derbyshire and the influence it had on his life and writing. Gazetteer of sites, maps and photographs.